DATE			

Strange
NEW SPECIES

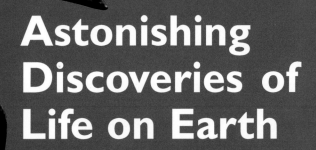

Astonishing Discoveries of Life on Earth

Elin Kelsey

MAPLE
TREE
PRESS

Maple Tree Press Inc.
51 Front Street East, Suite 200, Toronto, Ontario M5E 1B3
www.mapletreepress.com

Distributed in Canada by Raincoast Books
9050 Shaughnessy Street, Vancouver, British Columbia V6P 6E5

Distributed in the United States by Publishers Group West
1700 Fourth Street, Berkeley, California 94710

Dedication

For Esmé, Kip, Lucas, Matthias, Sylvie, Marielle, Fiona, Alanna, and Katherine — a celebration of the world for you.

Cataloguing in Publication Data

Kelsey, Elin
  Strange new species : astonishing discoveries of life on earth / Elin Kelsey.
Includes index.
ISBN 1-897066-31-7 (bound). — ISBN 1-897066-32-5 (pbk.)

  1. Biology — Juvenile literature. 2. Species — Juvenile literature.
3. Discoveries in science — Juvenile literature. I. Title.
QH48.K45 2005   j578   C2005-901169-6

Design: Blair Kerrigan/Glyphics

We acknowledge the financial support of the Canada Council for the Arts, the Ontario Arts Council, the Government of Canada through the Book Publishing Industry Development Program (BPIDP), and the Government of Ontario through the Ontario Media Development Corporation's Book Initiative for our publishing activities.

ONTARIO ARTS COUNCIL
CONSEIL DES ARTS DE L'ONTARIO

Printed in China

A   B   C   D   E   F

Contents

Foreword

Most people believe that our natural world is well documented, and it is true that identifying large living things new to science is a rare event nowadays. Today, most researchers discover new species by studying the world's museum collections, looking at animal and plant specimens collected long ago on expeditions to far and hostile places. What happened to the romance and adventure of the explorations of famous nineteenth-century naturalists? Well, my story demonstrates that there is still room for the old-fashioned species hunt in some corners of the world.

Before settling in Brazil, I had specialized in studying the fruits and monkeys of the northeastern Amazon. The wildlife of this area is well known. Illustrated field guides — including my own, describing the fruits and seeds of the woody plants of the area — mean that anyone can easily identify a mammal, bird, reptile, amphibian, or tree species they might spot in that region. Like many of you reading this book, I was convinced that most of the species of the world's tropical forests had been discovered and studied.

That idea changed totally for me on a day in 1996 when a milk-powder can was delivered to my halfway house for orphaned monkeys in Manaus, a boomtown in the central Brazilian Amazon. The can emitted a flurry of high-pitched shrieks. I opened it . . . and looked into the vivid eyes of the cutest little creature I had ever seen. Someone had brought us a tiny monkey the size of my finger — a species of monkey completely new to science.

This one monkey changed my life for good. I immediately sailed out to find the land the tiny primate came from, somewhere along the thousands of kilometres of the Madeira River. By the time I finally found the monkey's relatives in the wild, I had identified at least seven other primates new to science. Had I stumbled into a lost paradise overlooked by naturalists?

My eyes were opened to how rivers act as barriers between species of flightless animals, particularly monkeys — and I no longer held my old assumptions about finding new species. So I started a series of boat surveys sailing far up the main tributaries of the mighty Amazon River — rivers with romantic names like the Madeira, Purús, Juruá, Branco, Negro, and Tapajós. And there I found more undiscovered paradises, places that science had barely touched. Like islands in the ocean, the high dryland rain forests separated by rivers each seemed to have their own unique species makeup. Amazingly, they also included more new species, in animal groups such as tapir, deer, peccary, anteater, agouti, paca, dwarf porcupine, coati, jaguar, manatee, and dolphin.

As you read this book, your journey of discovery will reveal that it's not only the Amazon that is home to new species — your exploration will include Vietnam, India, Madagascar, and the Andean region, among others. And what about the deep sea? Or even your own back yard? I hope — and would not be surprised if — this book is just the start of the journey.

Marc G.M. van Roosmalen, Ph.D.
Manaus, Brazil

Strange New Life

A whale no one has ever seen. A deep-sea dragon discovered. An organism that could live on Mars. Do these discoveries sound like science fiction? Try science fact. They are just a few of the spectacular new species recently identified. Scientists are discovering more new species today — thousands each year — than at any other time in history.

In this book you'll find as many new ideas as animals and plants. Each discovery of a new life form challenges science to look at familiar species in new ways. Keep your eyes peeled for *Hot Debates* as you read on to uncover the latest species riddles. A *Glossary* and list of Web resources at the end of the book will help you take the discoveries farther.

Why are so many new species turning up? The field of genetic research is exploding with remarkable new ways to explore life on Earth. Thanks to DNA analysis (see page 16) and faster, more powerful computers, biologists can identify new species by examining their genetic codes, and can study relationships between species in ways they only dreamed of a decade ago.

New technologies also open up the frontiers of new species discovery. Remotely operated vehicles allow scientists to explore the deepest parts of the ocean. Pocket-sized global positioning units help them safely find their way to remote places where vast numbers of plants, animals, and other species live.

In these pages, you'll meet scientists who search for new species using everything from high-tech microscopes to spaghetti strainers. Some explore the mountain forests of Central America or the deserts of Mongolia. Others uncover new species in their own back yards.

Believe it or not, most of the world's species have not yet been identified. Could you uncover a brand new species? With millions yet to be discovered, there's a real chance you might.

SpecieStats

- Number of known species worldwide today is 1.7 million.
- Researchers estimate that between 5 and 100 million new species still await discovery.

Spot

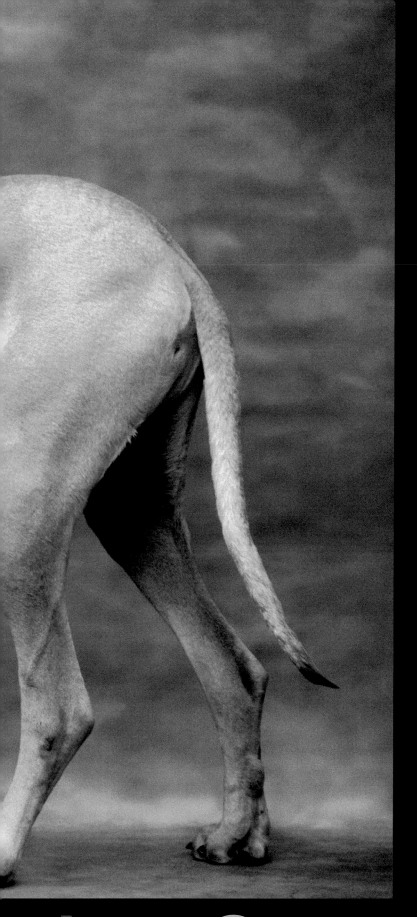

What is a species? You might not have known it, but you've been identifying them since you were a little kid. Two-year-olds say "doggy" whether they see a Great Dane or a bulldog, because no matter how big or small, how sleek or hairy, dogs look and act a lot alike. In the same way, biologists classify all dogs as the species *Canis domesticus*, because different dog breeds share physical characteristics and are similar enough to breed with each other to produce young. Figuring out if something is a new species, however, is usually not so easy.

The search for new species is all about the details. After all, the word "specific" and the word "species" are related. So let's get specific — just turn the page.

A Papillon and a Great Dane

the Species

Research Notes

Want to discover a new species? You'll have much better luck if you go looking for bugs rather than birds. Millions of insects are still undiscovered; most birds have been identified. Check the lists below for the total number of species scientists have identified so far for just a few of your favorite groups of animals and plants. Remember, these are estimates as of the year 2005. The numbers constantly change as new species are discovered and others are lost to extinction.

Bird: Cardinal

Birds
Class: Aves
Known species: more than 10,000
Note: Most of the world's bird species have been identified.
Look for:
• feathers and beaks
• babies that hatch from eggs
• wings for flying

Amphibians
Class: Amphibia
Known species: 4,200
Note: Frogs, toads, newts, and salamanders are all amphibians.
Look for animals that:
• spend at least part of their lives in water
• lay their eggs in water
• breathe through gills (just as fish do) when they are young
• have soft skin that easily absorbs water

Amphibian: Red Eft

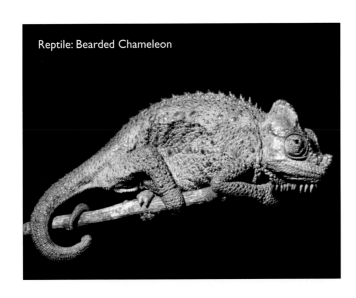
Reptile: Bearded Chameleon

Reptiles
Class: Reptilia
Known species: Nearly 8,000
Note: Lizards, snakes, tuataras, crocodiles, and turtles are all reptiles.
Look for animals that:
- lay leathery eggs on land
- have dry, scaly skin

Insect: Tiger Beetle

Insects
Class: Insecta
Known species: 751,000
Note: Scientists believe the number of insects on Earth may be as many as 30 million.
Look for:
- small, segmented bodies without backbones
- 3 pairs of legs
- usually 2 pairs of wings

Mammal: Gorilla

Mammals
Class: Mammalia
Known species: more than 4,600
Note: The big ones are well-described but many new species of tiny mammals are yet to be discovered.
Look for:
- hair — all mammals have hair at some stage in their life cycle
- mothers who nurse their young with milk

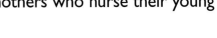

Research Notes ... *continued*

Flowering Plant: Potato

Flowering Plants
Phylum: Magnoliophyta
Known species: more than 230,000
Look for:
- plants that produce seeds in specialized reproductive organs called flowers

Fungi: Chanterelle Waxy Cap

Fungi
Kingdom: Fungi
Known species: more than 72,000
Note: Fungi take many forms. Some familiar ones include:
- mushrooms and toadstools
- yeasts

Marine Fish: Clown Fish

Marine Fishes
"Marine fish" is a common name that includes several scientific classes.
Number of known species: 15,300
Note: Thanks to the ongoing Census of Marine Life (see page 36), an average of three new species of marine fishes have been identified each week since the year 2000.
Look for:
- paired fins
- gills for breathing

Scientists also group species by ecosystems. Here are two ecosystems that are teeming with life: coral reefs and tropical rain forests.

Coral Reefs
Known species: 93,000
Note: Scientists believe there may be as many as 3 million coral reef species. Coral reefs are the richest ecosystem in the ocean. Nearly 25% of all marine life depends upon them for survival, yet coral reefs make up only a very small part of the world's oceans — far less than 1% of the vast ocean floor. Because of this, coral reefs are often called the rain forests of the sea.

Tropical Rain Forests
Known species: around 750,000
Note: Tropical rain forests cover only 7% of the total dry surface of the Earth, yet many scientists think they are home to 50% of the total number of species on our planet.

Coral Reef

Tropical Rain Forest

Remember, most species on Earth have not yet been identified and there are many more groups than those listed here. Also, these numbers constantly change as new species are discovered and others are lost to extinction.

The Name Game

Try to imagine a time when there were no microscopes, when no one understood blood circulation, gravity, or the solar system — when people didn't even know that the world was round. That's what life was like when Artistotle lived in the fourth century BC (384 to 322 BC). Yet this brilliant observer of nature described more than 500 different species, including shellfish, insects, birds, reptiles, and quadrupeds (four-legged animals).

For hundreds of years, scientists named new species based on descriptive characteristics suggested by Aristotle.

By the eighteenth century, 20,000 species were known to science, and the name game was getting out of hand. Some names had grown to twelve words or longer. Even more confusing, scientists sometimes used different words to describe the same thing. In 1757, Carl Linnaeus, a Swedish doctor and botanist, solved these problems by creating a system to name and classify all life.

Who has the oldest name in the world? If you're talking scientific names, there's a good chance a green sea turtle would be in the running . . . or the swimming! Green sea turtles have been called *Chelonia mydas* (which means "turtle from the sea" in ancient Greek) ever since Greek philosopher Artistotle named this as a new species 2,300 years ago.

The scientific classification system, or *taxonomy*, created by Carl Linnaeus (above) is still used by scientists today.

Species Explosion

Like Aristotle, Linnaeus assigned all living things into two groups or kingdoms — animals and plants. But as more new and unusual species were discovered, Linnaeus's system had to change to represent them. In the 1960s, the kingdoms of bacteria, fungi, and protista (one-celled organisms) were added. And just since you were born, the explosion of weird and wonderful new microscopic species has demanded another major revamping of scientific classification. Today, scientists organize all species into three super-kingdoms called domains. Two of these — Archaea and Bacteria — describe incredible forms of microscopic life that are nothing like the plants and animals Linnaeus knew.

Change Is the Name of the Game

Growing up in the nineteenth century, Charles Darwin (seen here at age 7 in 1816) delighted in collecting minerals, insects, coins, stamps, and other odd bits. In 1859, this young British naturalist announced his daring new theory of Natural Selection in his book *The Origin of Species*. Darwin wrote, "species have changed, and are still slowly changing." One of the biggest ideas in the history of the science, Darwin's theory changed the world.

Linnaeus's Classification System

Linnaeus's classification system has been updated over time and today it assigns every known living organism — about 1.75 million of them — to a kingdom, phylum, subphylum, class, order, family, genus, and species. Here's your official scientific name according to current Linnaean taxonomy:

Kingdom **Animalia** (animals)
Phylum **Chordata** (chordates)
Subphylum **Vertebrata** (vertebrates)
Class **Mammalia** (mammals)
Order **Primates** (primates)
Family **Hominidae** (man-like primates)
Genus **Homo** (human)
Species **sapiens** (wise)

That's *Homo sapiens* for short. You share the same scientific species name with every person on Earth. Keep your eyes open for other two-word "scientific names" — the genus and species — as you read through this book. Scientific names are in the ancient languages of Latin or Greek so that, no matter what language scientists normally use to communicate, they know they're talking about the same species.

After traveling to the Galapagos Islands off South America, and seeing the wealth of strange new wildlife (like this blue-footed booby), Charles Darwin developed a convincing argument about how species change over time.

▼

Darwin's book *The Origin of Species* was published in 1859. It caused such a stir, it sold out the day it was printed. It has been reprinted and sold in bookstores ever since that day!

It's All in the Genes

For more than 250 years, scientists have been using the following clues to help them classify new species:

- What it looks like (morphology)
- Where it lives in the world (range)
- How it acts (behavior)
- What it eats and what habitat it lives in (habitat requirements)

Scientists followed a general rule: if they couldn't tell members of different groups apart, then they didn't treat them as different species. But DNA analysis challenges this idea.

Whether you're a kid, a virus, or a tulip, your cells contain DNA (deoxyribonucleic acid), made up of genes that transmit information from one generation to the next. Each gene stores thousands of pieces of genetic "code," and the endless combinations of these codes create Earth's amazing diversity of life forms.

High-speed computers can analyze any creature's DNA. So a species' genetic code is a powerful new clue to be added to the list used in species classification. It can help scientists decide if a species is new or not.

In 2003, scientists at Wayne State University in Michigan studied human and chimpanzee genes, and reported that 99.4% of the most important DNA sites on the genes are

DNA is so tiny, you can only see its twisted structure with a powerful microscope. If all the genetic information contained in your body was written in words, it would fill 800 dictionary-sized books.

David Wake, a scientist at the University of California, Berkeley, used protein and DNA analysis to study the common California slender salamander *Batrachoseps attenuatus*. He found that what was thought to be a single species is really a complex of many different species. The discovery of new populations has brought the slender salamander count to 20 species.

identical. These researchers believe that, with such a close relationship, chimps and humans should be re-classified together in the same genus *Homo*. Other researchers are not so sure. Depending upon precisely which genetic differences scientists look at, the similarity may be only 95–98%. Not enough, they argue, to change the classification.

Genetic analysis takes the search for new species to a new level. For the first time in history, scientists can detect new microscopic species entirely by the gene sequences found in air, water, and soil samples. In 2004, researchers discovered 1,800 new species and 1.2 million new genes in a single water sample from the Sargasso Sea.

Should Chimpanzees, like this one, be re-classified into the same scientific genus as humans? That's just one of the many hot new species debates.

Part the dense, green foliage in front of your face and take a look around. Before you, mighty trees reach high into the forest canopy ten stories above the ground. Tiny birds forage in the leaves and among the mosses, ferns, and orchids. Spiders and insects crawl in front of your face. Sweat trickles down your back. Welcome to the rain forest, the richest, most diverse ecosystem on Earth.

Suddenly, a sound like distant traffic cuts through the buzzing of the bugs. A tropical downpour! You scramble for your rain poncho, your shoulders stinging from the force of the drops. It's impossible to see through the torrent of driving rain. How many new species share this amazingly wild, green, wet world? Turn the page and see.

Rain forest, Borneo, Asia

the Rain Forest

Monkeyshines

What kinds of pets live in your neighborhood? The back yard of Marc van Roosmalen's South American home in Brazil is sometimes full of orphaned monkeys swinging in and out of trouble, some of them new species waiting to be named by science. Marc is a primatologist (a scientist who studies primates, which include apes, monkeys, and lemurs).

Sometimes the most amazing animals turn up on his doorstep. In 1996, a river trader delivered a baby pygmy marmoset, a mouse-sized infant that turned out to be a brand new species called the black-headed sagui dwarf, or *Callithrix humilis* (see below). More exciting still, Marc believes it represents a whole new group, or genus, of monkeys — the first to be discovered since 1904.

To prove the tiny monkey was a new species, Marc needed to find more of them. All he knew was that the monkey had been found on a boat coming down the Rio Madeira, a river 3,200 kilometres

Primates have been closely studied, so finding a new species has been quite rare. This baby black-headed sagui dwarf is a new species of marmoset, and the world's second smallest monkey. ▼

HOUSE CALLS

Animals may be unknown to science, but familiar to people who share the rain forest with them. So Marc often visits remote villages looking for suspected new species among the local pets. He'll adopt a rare animal (maybe trading some rice or chicken for it) and give it a new home at the research center, where he can learn more about the way it lives. Only when the animal dies of natural causes does he perform scientific study to prove that it is a new species.

(2,000 mi.) long. Finding the little primates took him more than a year of hiking around the jungle, surviving in the wild by eating what monkeys eat and imitating the behaviors of the animals he observed.

Marc believes the Amazon is full of new species, including more than 15 new primates. He and other scientists argue that the discovery of so many new primate species is evidence of just how little we understand about the Amazon — the world's largest rain forest — and proves how important it is to conserve it.

Marc van Roosmalen has scientifically classified at least seven new monkey species and a whole new genus. In 2002 alone, Marc and his colleagues named two new species — *Callicebus bernhardi* (above left) and *Callicebus stephennashi* (above right).

Marc van Roosmalen

Marc follows his curiosity through the Amazon rain forest, his senses on full alert, traveling alone because he sees more that way. As a boy in Holland, he cared for the lizards, snakes, and frogs he collected. Today, Marc is deeply committed to conserving nature, which earned him recognition as a *TIME* magazine Hero for the Planet. Within your lifetime, he has identified many never-before-seen species of primates, a species of peccary (wild pig), a lost cousin of the Brazil nut tree, and an anthurium plant with leaves bigger than elephant ears. He has also found what he believes to be new species of manatee and river dolphin.

Leaping Lemurs!

A mouse lemur (above) is the size of a chipmunk and weighs less than a sandwich, but the discovery of three new species of mouse lemur is *gigantic* news. Madagascar, off Africa's east coast, is the only place in the world where lemurs are found. The three newly discovered species live in the dry, dense forests along the island's west coast.

21

Tropical Treasure Troves

▲ These new species of "stinky" frogs from Vietnam smell quite bad. Their body odor may repel mosquitoes and larger predators.

Stinky frogs and poisonous snakes may sound like ingredients for a witch's brew, but they're actually just a few of the unusual new species Bob Murphy has discovered in Vietnam. Tons of rain and a year-round growing season turn tropical rain forests into the greenest places you can imagine. Vietnam's rain forests are a paradise for identifying new species.

Bob is a herpetologist (a scientist who studies reptiles and amphibians) and he specializes in cryptic species — species that look alike but are genetically different. In the case of the stinky frogs, Bob was lucky enough to be in a logging camp in Vietnam during frog-breeding season. The variety of frog calls he heard every morning and evening convinced him to collect frogs for DNA analysis in his lab. His findings were worth the effort: what had been classified as a single species of frog turned out to be three separate species. Thanks to more collection trips at different times of the year, the number of new species of stinky frogs from Vietnam has now reached eight — and that's just the *stinky* frogs. Over just a few years, the number of frog species identified in Vietnam doubled to more than 160.

There are so many species to discover that Bob feels like an eighteenth-century explorer, but instead of a lantern he carries a high-tech flashlight. A hand-held GPS (global positioning system) unit provides him with maps and information about his location anywhere in the world, and portable canisters of liquid nitrogen preserve specimens in even the most remote places. Back at the lab, he uses up-to-the-minute technology to make a closer inspection of animals he has collected. Only through DNA analysis, for example, was Bob able to determine that thick "adult" and thin "baby" coral snakes were actually two completely different snake species.

Researchers thought that these two coral snakes were an adult (left) and baby (right) of the same species. But, although one was much thicker than the other, they were both the same length. They had males and females of both thin and thick snakes, so that wasn't the difference. DNA analysis showed that, even though they look the same, these two snakes are different species.

More than 50% of the world's plant and animal species live in the just 7% of the Earth's land surface that makes up tropical rain forests, like Khe Moi, Vietnam (above).

These horns are from the saola, a species recently discovered in Vietnam. This antelope-like hoofed animal is so rare that it has never been photographed alive.

Bob Murphy

Bob (center, above) has always loved the outdoors. When he was young, he would often go wandering in the woods near his home, coming home rather disheveled. His initial intense fascination was with mammals, but he became completely absorbed in learning about marine invertebrates, especially snails and crabs. Although he always wanted to be a biologist, his passion for amphibians and reptiles did not develop until his last year of university. One trip to the Mojave Desert of southern California, and he was completely hooked. "Dr. Bob" is the Senior Curator of Herpetology at the Royal Ontario Museum.

Small Change

Balance a dime on the tip of your finger, and you've got the perfect platform for one of the world's smallest lizards. Even its name printed here, *Eleutherodactylus iberia*, is three times longer than its 10 mm (0.4 in.) body. Alberto Estrada, a Cuban scientist, discovered this new species living under the leaf litter in a humid Cuban rain forest while he was searching for a rare species of woodpecker.

Listen Up!

Next time you wake up at sunrise, poke your head outside and listen. How many different bird songs can you recognize? Scientist Mark Robbins can recognize nearly 2,000 bird species just by the sound of their voices. Thanks to this amazing ability, Mark has discovered four new species of birds.

Ornithologist Mark Robbins (above left) uses his binoculars to scan a remote area in Ecuador for new species.

Because most of the world's species of birds have already been identified, Mark looks for new species in remote South American tropical forests where few, if any, people have ever been. Like islands in the ocean, forests atop high, isolated mountains often have unique bird communities that just might include species unknown to science.

Some of Mark's study sites are home to more than 300 different bird species, so it takes him several days to sort out the sounds of all the birds he can hear. As soon as he has a good idea of the birds he is already familiar with, he tries to filter out their sounds to listen for the quieter, less obvious voices. It's like listening for a new kid whispering in a school yard crowded with the shouts of familiar friends.

Birdcalls provide important clues about new species, especially for birds that sound different but look alike. Jessica Young was a university student in the United States in the 1980s. She listened to tapes of the northern sage grouse *Centrocercus urophasianus* for a biology project. The calls recorded near Gunnison, Colorado, sounded so unique that she suspected they belonged to a different species. Over the next decade, Jessica and other scientists recorded and studied sage grouse vocalizations, behaviors, anatomy, and genetic makeup. She earned her Ph.D. and became a university professor while making the case that, according to all the concepts of what makes a species, these birds were unique. In 2000 it became official. A new species, the Gunnison sage grouse *Centrocercus minimus,* was named.

Male sage grouse (like this one in full mating strut) are famous for their mating calls, which can be heard a couple of kilometres away.

Mark Robbins

Mark's first love was reptiles. When he was eight years old, he would exchange snakes he collected in his neighborhood for exotic reptiles from other parts of the world. He became obsessed and passionate about birds when he was 13 and, by the time he started university, he was taking frequent trips to watch birds in Mexico. Mark continues to make a couple of trips a year surveying birds in a variety of countries, and is now the Collections Manager for Ornithology at the Natural History Museum, University of Kansas.

A Bird in the Hand

Does Mark Robbins know where he is likely to find a new species? Sometimes. A few years ago, he co-led an expedition to Mount Roraima in South America. There he discovered what might turn out to be new species of pygmy-owl. Pygmy-owls had not yet been found on Roraima, but Mark's prediction that they might be living there was based on what he knew about the type of habitat pygmy-owls prefer.

Other times, birds show up in surprising locations. Mark and his colleague Gary Rosenberg never expected to find the chestnut-bellied cotinga *Doliornis remseni* that they discovered high up a mountain in Ecuador. They couldn't believe their eyes when they saw what looked like a bird usually seen thousands of kilometres away. When they finally got a close look at the "surprise," they found that it looked like a different-colored version of its southern relative.

Searching High and Low

If you like to watch birds, you're in good company. Bird-watching is one of the world's fastest growing hobbies. With so many people on the lookout for birds, it isn't surprising that birds are the best-identified group of animals on Earth. Only two or three new bird species are discovered each year, and these are usually hard-to-spot species that live in very remote places.

It Takes a Village

The discovery of a new pygmy owl species in Guyana took the team effort of researchers from the University of Guyana and the Smithsonian Institution, and volunteers from Kako Village. Together, they cut trails and carried heavy research gear up the steep, muddy slopes of Mount Roraima. Mark hopes that speaking to kids — both at home in Kansas and in his "homes away from home" in South America — will help them realize the many ways that they and their families can help find and conserve wildlife.

Chestnut-bellied cotingas are usually found far from the mountains in Ecuador where Mark Robbins and Gary Rosenberg found this one. Their good memory for birds helped the scientists make this unusual discovery.

Worth the Wait

When can you be sure you have found a new species? Sometimes making sure can take months, or even years. Finding, or *collecting*, an animal is just an early step in the scientific process of identifying, or *describing*, a new species. For Mark Robbins, it starts with comparing a sound recording of a pygmy-owl's call with recordings of the calls of other birds. Then the bird itself is compared with others suspected to be the same species. Finally, genetic tests reveal the bird's DNA sequence, which is compared with that of other pygmy-owls. It's the last step that can take a long time — scientists need to analyze all the other species that might be related to the new discovery.

New Species

Unfortunately, scientists aren't the only ones eager to find new species. Rare and unusual animals fetch a high price from collectors who purchase them illegally. Whenever scientists discover a unique new species, they have to freely share information with other scientists. But how do they make sure it doesn't end up causing the animal to be a target for black-market dealers?

Examiner Barry Baker takes a skin sample. Using DNA and other methods of analysis, scientists can prove that a drop of blood or a piece of skin could only have come from one species of animal in the entire world.

You might have heard of crime scene investigation (CSI) and forensics labs, where science is used to help solve crimes. Animal conservationists have the National Fish and Wildlife Forensics Laboratory — a high-tech lab devoted to solving crimes against animals. The same DNA tests that help scientists determine if an animal is a new species are useful for identifying and reducing wildlife crimes. Recently, the lab was successful in helping to convict a businesswoman for the possession of 130 luxury shawls made illegally from hairs of endangered Tibetan antelopes.

DNA analysis also provides important information to determine which habitats should be protected by law. Fringe-toed lizards, for instance, are found in the southwestern US and Mexico. Some are endangered; others are not. By taking tiny samples of a tail or toe, researchers can tell what species it is without harming the individual animal.

In the evidence room of the National Fish and Wildlife Forensics Laboratory are illegal items that represent millions of dollars — and the lives of many endangered animal species.

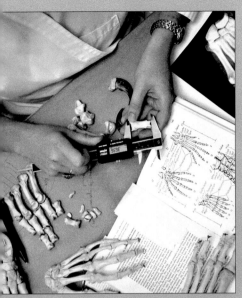

As in any crime lab, evidence of illegal hunting is collected and recorded. Here, bones are measured to determine species.

Bob Murphy (see page 23) has determined that each species of fringe-toed lizard depends on a different dune system. His research shows that, to protect the range of different fringe-toed lizard species, you need to protect different sorts of dunes by making it illegal to damage them.

And big news for elephant conservation: researchers from the University of California at San Diego have released DNA evidence confirming that African elephants are really three different species — the African Forest Elephant, the African Savannah Elephant, and the West African Elephant. African elephant populations have been rapidly declining in the past century. Elephants' survival has been challenged by ongoing destruction of their habitats and attacks by ivory poachers, who kill elephants for their tusks. Thanks to stronger anti-poaching programs, the number of elephants has started to increase in the past decade. But now some southern African countries want to reduce their numbers. The discovery that they are dealing with three species argues against doing this. Instead of there simply being 500,000 African elephants, there will be a smaller number of each kind, making all three species more threatened and more in need of legal protection.

You may be able to recognize these two types of elephants — African (left) and Asian (right). Now, a team of African and American researchers have DNA evidence suggesting that there are actually three separate species of African elephants.

Insect Hide 'n' Seek

Who says pillowcases are just for wrapping around pillows? Stuffing insects into pillowcases on remote mountaintops is not unusual for Bob Anderson.

A scientist needs lots of fancy equipment to do the job, right? Not according to Bob Anderson, a beetle expert working at the Canadian Museum of Nature. Bob is a systematic entomologist (a scientist who classifies insects) with a passion for traveling to new areas in search of new species. When all of Bob's luggage, including his insect-collecting equipment, got lost on a trip to Panama, Bob didn't wait for the delivery of new supplies. Instead, he borrowed a pair of boots, some insect repellent, and a dozen fancy pillowcases. He boarded the charter plane that would fly him to a cloud forest, high atop one of Panama's most remote mountains. For the next week, Bob explored the forest floor, scooping up leaf litter in search of new species of beetles. What do you suppose he used to carry all those insects, twigs, bark, and leaves back to his camp? Fancy pillowcases!

Most insects live way up high or way down low — more than five stories up in the forest canopy or only a toddler's height from the forest floor. Entomologists (scientists who study insects) use many different methods to collect them. Some go gleaning, which means they pick insects off the leaves, just like birds do. Others spread large sheets beneath a tree and give the tree a mighty whack to jar its insect inhabitants loose. Still others catch insects on the fly by stretching sections of mosquito netting between two posts. Sometimes, a fog of insect spray is pumped high

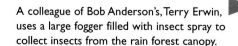
A colleague of Bob Anderson's, Terry Erwin, uses a large fogger filled with insect spray to collect insects from the rain forest canopy.

into the branches of trees. Insects killed by the spray rain down onto huge sheets suspended above the ground, enabling entomologists to identify species that live too high in the canopy to collect by hand.

Bob hunts for insects close to the ground. He scoops dead leaves and dirt from the forest floor and strains them through screen mesh to remove any rocks or chunks of wood. It takes him about half an hour to collect one sample of forest floor material, about enough to fill a pillowcase. He ties the pillowcase at the top and leaves it by the side of the trail until he comes back down the mountain. On a good day, Bob returns looking like Santa Claus, with ten overstuffed pillowcases slung across his back!

Scientist Stewart Peck uses his van to collect insect specimens. He mounts a fine mesh net on the front bumper where a snowplow would be attached. When he drives down old logging roads in Ontario, Canada, he nets about 10,000 bugs per hour.

RESEARCHER PROFILE

Bob Anderson

As a kid growing up in Ireland and Canada, Bob was always interested in natural history. Trips to museums and zoos were his favorite pastime, aside from exploring the local forests and fields around home. Bob's mother would cringe as she emptied his pockets, because she never knew what kinds of worms, bugs, and other creepy critters he would have stuffed in them. Bob is a research scientist at the Canadian Museum of Nature.

High Hopes for High Places

Bob discovers new species by looking in places no one has looked before. Many biologists work in tropical lowland rain forests, because each square metre (10 square ft.) can house more kinds of plants and animals than a square metre of any other habitat on Earth. But Bob prefers to look in tropical cloud forests on the tops of mountains. The species that live on top of one mountain are separated from species that live on the top of another. And separate places often mean separate species. Since there are a lot of mountains, Bob believes that large cloud forests may actually be home to more species than similarly sized areas of lowland rain forests. He hopes his studies will help to gain conservation protection for these biological hotspots.

31

A World of Insects

Bob Anderson is particularly interested in discovering more about the lives of a group of beetles known as weevils. On a six-week trip to Honduras, Central America, Bob visited 13 mountaintops and collected more than 26,000 weevils. Back at camp, and later in the museum lab, Bob sorted the weevils into their distinct forms. Almost each of the resulting 293 forms represents a new species of weevil.

Thousands of potential new species of insects sit in collection drawers at the Canadian Museum of Nature, awaiting study and naming. ▼

It takes a lot of time in the lab to carefully describe the characteristics that make a species unique. Bob has described and given names to only about 200 of the thousands of new species he has collected. Bob is so good at finding new species, he has five species and one genus of insects actually named after him. But he points out that you don't have to go to Central or South America to find something interesting and significant. In Canada, scientists have named 30,000 species of insects, but Bob believes there are at least 30,000 more that haven't been identified.

HOT DEBATE SUBWAY HOME TO NEW SPECIES OF MOSQUITO?

It's warm, it's damp, and it's full of prey for hungry mosquitoes. No, it's not the rain forest — it's the London Underground (subway system)! The mosquitoes that live there are believed to be the descendants of the species of mosquito *Culex pipiens* that entered the tunnels more than a hundred years ago when the Underground (nicknamed the Tube) was being dug. Some scientists believe the Tube mosquitoes' genetic makeup is so different from their ancestors that they are a new species. Others are not yet convinced. They agree the mosquitoes are on the way to becoming a new species, but argue that the Underground colony may

Bob Anderson's research camp includes a "bug lab" where Bob can separate insects from three or four samples a day. The lights over the funnels dry out the leaf litter inside, causing the insects living in it to burrow deeper and deeper — and into preserving alcohol below.

Globetrotting Bloodsuckers

The London Underground isn't the only transportation location where you'll find rapidly evolving mosquitoes. Mosquitoes are famous for their ability to evolve resistance to insecticides (chemicals that kill insects). A group of *Culex pipiens* from Africa are immune to certain kinds of insecticides. And, since they've followed people onto planes, trains, and boats, these extra-resistant mosquitoes have now spread to other parts of the world.

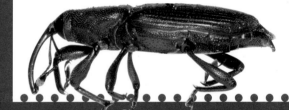

You Could be a Bug

Only half of the insect species in Canada have a name, and the folks at the Canadian Museum of Nature have come up with a clever way to name these bugs — and raise funds for new insect discoveries. You can donate $500 or more to their Nature Discovery Fund, and have a species named in your honor. Canadian writer Margaret Atwood was so taken with the idea, she named this Atwood palm weevil *Metamasius atwoodi* in honor of her favorite forest ecologist — her father, Dr. Carl Atwood!

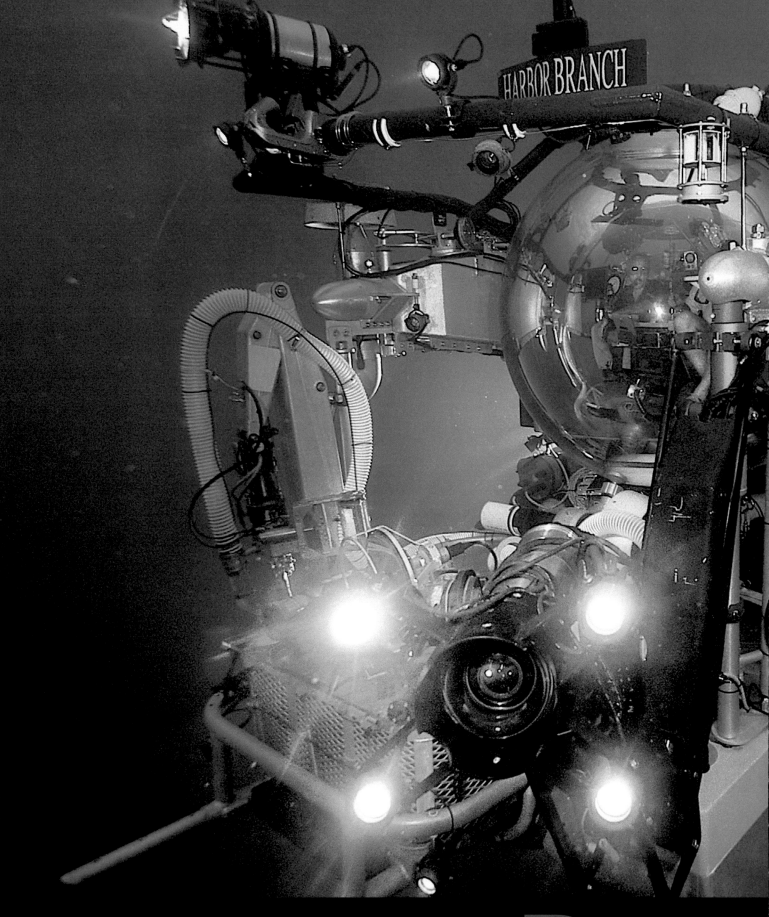

Imagine a dark region of the ocean where sunlight fades to blackness and plants can no longer grow. Welcome to the deep sea, a mysterious habitat that is even deeper than Mount Everest is tall. Because only the newest technology can go this deep, most deep sea species have never been seen or described.

No sunlight, no plants — you might think that this is not a good place to find new species. But think again! The deep sea is the largest habitat on Earth, and more animals may live in the deep sea than anywhere else. Scientists think that as many as 10 million deep-sea animal species are waiting in the depths to be discovered. So get ready to dive deep — and turn the page.

A manned submersible, Fort Pierce, Florida

into the Deep

Life Far Below

Beyond the northern shores of the Yukon and Alaska, isolated for tens of millions of years, the Canada Basin lies far beneath the ice-covered surface of the Arctic Ocean. What lives in the oldest, coldest waters in the world?

It's 3,800 metres (12,500 ft.) deep, completely surrounded by underwater mountain ridges. What new species lurk in the Canada Basin's deep, dark, icy waters? That's what a team of researchers from Canada, the US, and Russia are eager to discover. Equipped with ice breakers, remote-operated video cameras, and submersibles, they are probing one of the least accessible places on Earth.

This exciting project is part of the Census of Marine Life, an international effort to identify all ocean animal and plant species by 2010. Spurred by a 1995 report that human population growth might have devastating effects on the oceans' diverse life forms, scientists started the Census in 2000. That's ten years to study the oceans that cover 70% of the Earth's surface.

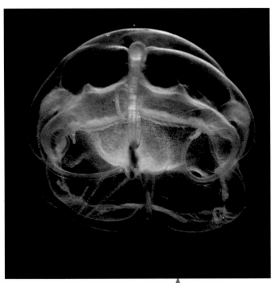

From this ghostly looking jellyfish ▲ to the collection of creatures found on an arctic shelf, deep arctic waters are home to a surprising variety of new species.

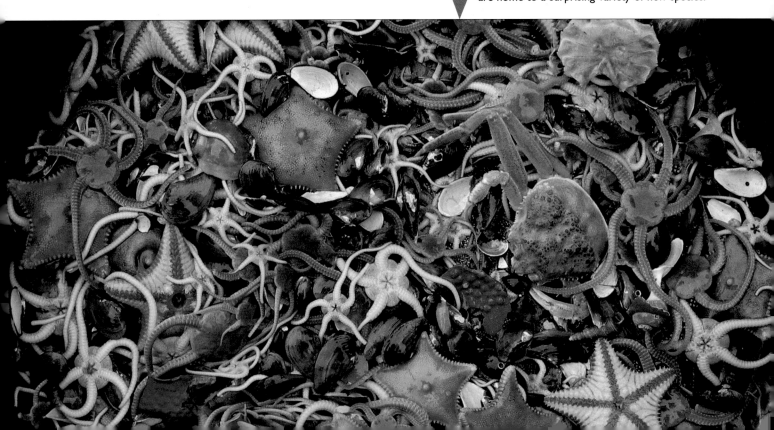

By 2004, scientists had identified thousands of new species, in addition to the 230,000 species of ocean plants and animals already known. And that was just as the phase of the Census studying microbes, the smallest sea life, was starting up. When that part is done, scientists expect the Census to have counted 20,000 species of fish and up to 1.98 million species of animals and plants.

Big Red

Like a giant red balloon measuring a metre (over 3 ft.) wide, this jellyfish, *Tiburonia granrojo* — the species name translates as "Big Red"— floats through the deep ocean off Hawaii, California, and Japan. Unlike most jellies, it has no tentacles. Instead, it uses its four to seven fleshy arms to capture food. Discovered and named by scientists of the Monterey Bay Aquarium Research Institute, *T. granrojo* differs from other jellies in such fundamental ways it had to be assigned to a whole new subfamily (Tiburoniinae).

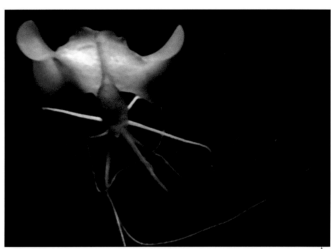

Scientists have identified about 280 species of squid. This large species — estimated to be 4 to 5 metres (13–16 ft.) in length — was encountered by a remotely operated vehicle (ROV) off the coast of Oahu, Hawaii. At a depth of 3,380 metres (11,090 ft.), that's as far down as many mountains are up!

Where is all Earth's water?

Virtually all of the water on the planet — 97.957% of it — is in the oceans. Of the rest, you might think that most is found in lakes and rivers, but only a tiny 0.036% of the Earth's water makes up these fresh-water resources. An amazing 45 times the amount of water found in lakes and rivers is iced up in glaciers and ice caps.

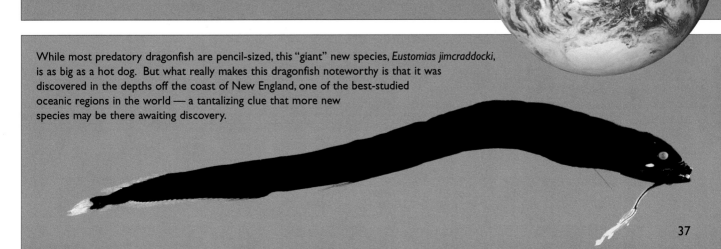

While most predatory dragonfish are pencil-sized, this "giant" new species, *Eustomias jimcraddocki*, is as big as a hot dog. But what really makes this dragonfish noteworthy is that it was discovered in the depths off the coast of New England, one of the best-studied oceanic regions in the world — a tantalizing clue that more new species may be there awaiting discovery.

Sending ROV-er to Fetch

It's hard work to launch the two-ton ROV *Ventana* from the research vessel in the open waters of Monterey Bay, California. After thousands of dives, the crew is well practiced at handling the ROV cable (which contains wires and optical fiber) so that it doesn't stretch or kink.

We know less about the deep sea than we know about the surface of Mars. It is a landscape so cold and dark, and under such extreme pressure, that humans cannot explore it directly. Instead, researchers at the Monterey Bay Aquarium rely on the "senses" of a multi-million-dollar remotely operated vehicle (ROV).

With its oversized lights and cameras, the ROV enables scientists to see far down beneath the surface. The ROV can also emit sonar — pulses of sound that produce sound pictures of the surrounding area.

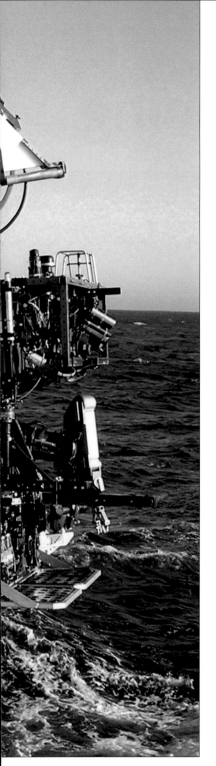

Probes on board the ROV test the water temperature and levels of oxygen and other chemicals. In fact, the information the ROV sends back seems so immediate that it's easy for researchers to forget that they are sitting safely at the surface, far away from the action. Once a scientist literally jumped from his seat when a school of giant squid the size of professional basketball players suddenly surrounded the ROV cameras!

Science sometimes means combining high-tech with low-tech. Floor-mop sponges mounted on the ROV's robotic arm protect these delicate sea whips during transport to the surface. ▼

The ROV often finds new species when it journeys deep into Monterey Bay. Some animals, like this *Saccopharynx lavenbergi*, defy imagination. Who could have thought up a human-sized fish that is almost all gulping, hinged mouth!

HOT DEBATE ## CRISIS IN THE RAIN FORESTS OF THE DEEP

We usually think of coral reefs as warm, shallow ecosystems, but it turns out that reefs as deep as 3.5 kilometres (2.2 mi.) also teem with thousands of new species. But many are being destroyed by commercial fishing faster than scientists can identify them. Fishing vessels drag trawls (huge nets armed with steel weights or heavy rollers) across the sea floor to catch shrimp and fish for our tables, smashing corals and sponges and ripping them from the depths. Many scientists believe the devastation of deep-sea corals by bottom trawlers is what is responsible for the decline of major fish populations, such as cod, that has put some fisheries out of business.

Sweeping and Straining

Chase a blob of gelatin around your dessert bowl and try to imagine how you would pick up an animal that oozy. Now imagine that your spoon is being held by a remote control arm several city blocks away! That's the challenge Ed Seidel and his colleagues experienced while collecting pom-pom anemones for the Monterey Bay Aquarium.

Before each dive of the ROV, Ed loves to prowl along the aisles of his neighborhood hardware store, examining hoses, pipes, filters, and gadgets in search of gizmos he can attach to the mini-submarine's robotic arms. Virtual reality technology allows the arms to mimic the pilot's arm movements, so tools made for humans are often a good fit. Ed found an ordinary metal dustpan that he thought would be ideal for scooping the delicate pom-pom anemones from the sandy sea floor. Of course sweeping up a pom-pom anemone is not as easy as tidying your kitchen floor. Pom-pom anemones change shape. They look like jumbo pancakes when they are in a current that carries tiny particles of food. But when food becomes scarce, they puff themselves up like underwater tumbleweeds and let the current carry them to better places to feed.

Even with a $3 dustpan, (left) you still need a million-dollar robotic arm attached to a multi-million-dollar mini-submarine to collect new species of deep sea animals. And it won't always work! The spaghetti strainer filched from the kitchen (right) did a better job — and its smooth surface kept the anemones from sticking. ▼

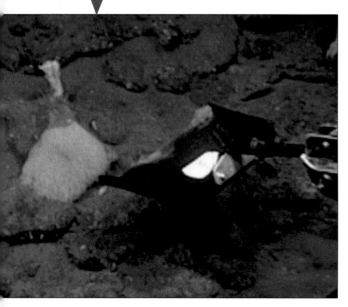

One of the exciting things about collecting new species of deep sea creatures is that you can't predict how they will behave. When the robotic arm of the ROV tried to scoop up pom-pom anemones, the current blew the anemones right off the dustpan. Luckily, one of the engineers had an idea. He disappeared into the ship's galley and returned with a colander used for draining spaghetti. Off came the dustpan, on went the colander, and down went the ROV for another try. To everyone's delight, the colander provided a protective shell that kept the pom-pom anemones from being washed away by the current, while the holes in its sides allowed water and sand to pass through easily.

The jelly-like pom-pom anemone *Liponema brevicornis* lives hundreds of stories down, down, down . . . on the sandy bottom of a deep ocean canyon off the central coast of California.

Eruptions of New Species

French scientists have just discovered hundreds of new species of corals, sponges, sea fans, and other invertebrate animals (some dating back to the age of the dinosaurs) living on extinct underwater volcanoes off the coast of New Zealand. Each volcano appears to be home to its own unique population of species. That's exciting news — especially given that only five of the world's 30,000 deep-sea mountains have been explored so far.

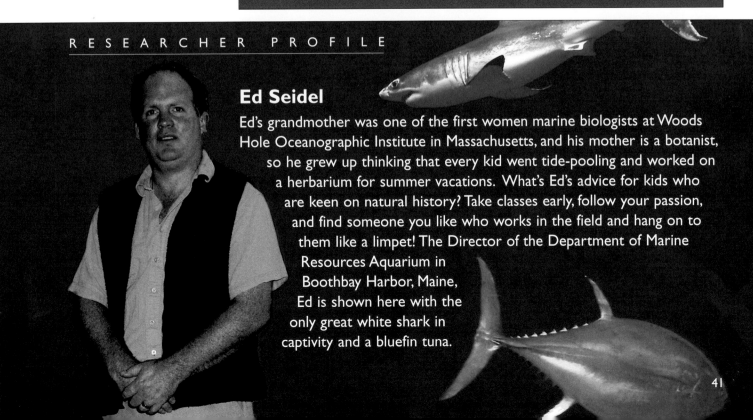

RESEARCHER PROFILE

Ed Seidel

Ed's grandmother was one of the first women marine biologists at Woods Hole Oceanographic Institute in Massachusetts, and his mother is a botanist, so he grew up thinking that every kid went tide-pooling and worked on a herbarium for summer vacations. What's Ed's advice for kids who are keen on natural history? Take classes early, follow your passion, and find someone you like who works in the field and hang on to them like a limpet! The Director of the Department of Marine Resources Aquarium in Boothbay Harbor, Maine, Ed is shown here with the only great white shark in captivity and a bluefin tuna.

Deep-Sea Tanks

An aquarium exhibit provides a rare peek at the beautiful, hidden world of deep-sea species. Every year, about 1.8 million people visit the 550 different species on exhibit at the Monterey Bay Aquarium.

The Monterey Bay Aquarium is the first place in the world to exhibit deep-sea species. Ed Seidel and his colleagues had to do a lot of experimenting to figure out how to build tanks that can keep deep-sea animals alive and healthy. The exhibits were fitted with chillers to keep the water just a few degrees above freezing. The lights were covered with red plastic gels to simulate the inky darkness of the ocean depths. Tremendous pressure exists under water that is kilometres deep; however, they couldn't build exhibits that replicated that pressure yet could still be opened for cleaning and feeding.

Most of the animals did just fine in unpressurized conditions. But three months after they joined the exhibit, the animals known as predatory tunicates started dying. Ed and his colleagues went back through their list of deep-sea conditions: cold water, darkness, high pressure. Could the lack of high pressure be the cause of death?

Careful examination of other animals in the exhibit provided an important clue. To Ed's surprise, the fine hairs on the tentacles of animals called droopy sea pens looked as if they were melting. It turns out that water at deep-sea depths contains less than 10% of the oxygen found in water at the surface. The extra oxygen in the surface-level water was what the sea pens and tunicates couldn't handle. It was super-oxidizing their

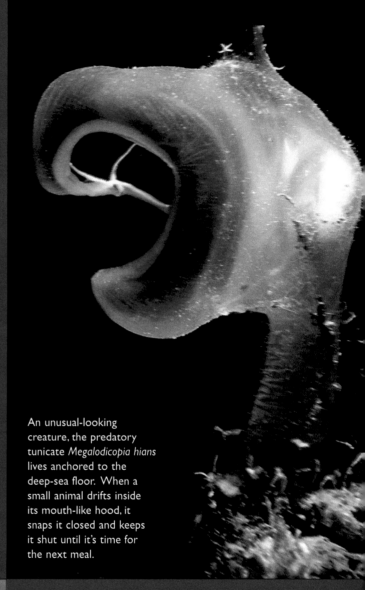

An unusual-looking creature, the predatory tunicate *Megalodicopia hians* lives anchored to the deep-sea floor. When a small animal drifts inside its mouth-like hood, it snaps it closed and keeps it shut until it's time for the next meal.

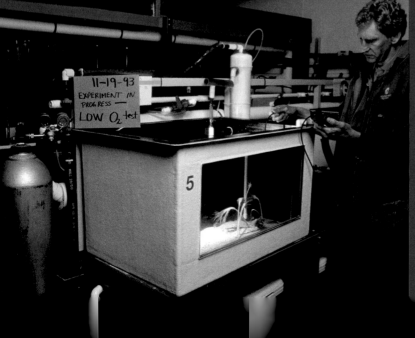

tissues and killing them. By bubbling nitrogen into the tank, the aquarium staff were able to create a low-oxygen system. The revised exhibit works so well, the tunicates are not only surviving but are producing larvae.

When researchers at the Monterey Bay Aquarium found that there was too much oxygen in the water of the deep-sea exhibit, they experimented with ways to make the water a better home for the droopy sea pens and predatory tunicates.

Deep, Dark, Toxic, and HOT!

It's easy to imagine a sleeping giant resting on these rocky pillows. These rounded rocks are formed when lava erupts underwater.

When the gigantic plates that form the Earth's crust move, they create cracks and crevices in the ocean floor. Seawater seeps into these openings, is heated by the molten rock that lies beneath the crust, and spews back out as a vent of super-hot, mineral-rich water.

Compared to their invertebrate relatives — like clams and other bivalves that evolved more than 50 million years ago — vent species are fairly recently evolved. Fossil evidence indicates that these vent shrimp have been around a mere 25 million years!

Some vent species, like crabs, are remarkably tolerant of temperature changes and may be able to walk between vents that are not too far apart. Polychaete worms and amphipods cling to crab shells and might hitch a ride.

What do firewalkers and deep-sea vent animals have in common? They're both capable of hopping across surfaces as hot as 426°C (800°F). But unlike firewalkers, who touch the stones and quickly move on, deep-sea vent animals live in a boiling billow of water and molten rock. When your parents were young, no one imagined that creatures could live in these conditions. Since scientists first visited a deep-sea vent in 1979, 700 new species have been described from this strange habitat.

Deep-sea vents are spread along underwater mountain ranges like the East Pacific Rise and the Mid-Atlantic Ridge. It's not too surprising that vent species in the Pacific are different from those in the Atlantic. Yet even the vent communities that share the same ocean may be isolated by hundreds of kilometres of ocean floor, like far-flung islands on the bottom of the sea.

Tubeworms ▶

Most marine invertebrates (animals without backbones) reproduce by releasing eggs or sperm, or even larva, into the water. These microscopic organisms are too tiny to choose where they are going. So how do deep-sea vent babies travel the incredible distances that separate one vent from another? As a scientist who studies population genetics, Diane Poehls hopes to find out.

◀

Clams, mussels, tubeworms — animals you would recognize from a shallow tidepool — can also be found in a completely foreign environment at the bottom of the sea. Current research suggests that the ancestors of deep-sea vent animals lived in shallow waters and that, over time, they populated the deep.

One Species' Poison

Deep-sea vent communities take chemicals that would be toxic to us from their environments and convert them into food energy. There are also a fantastic number of vent species that have adapted to live on "food falls" — debris such as coconuts or wood that sink to the bottom as they decompose. There is even a species of mussel specialized to live on "whale falls" — the carcasses of decomposing whales.

So tiny that it is photographed through a magnifying microscope, the larva of a deep-sea vent snail travels from one vent community to another. How? Diane Poehls studies the dominant currents that sweep along the oceanic ridges to determine if they might carry larvae to neighboring vents.

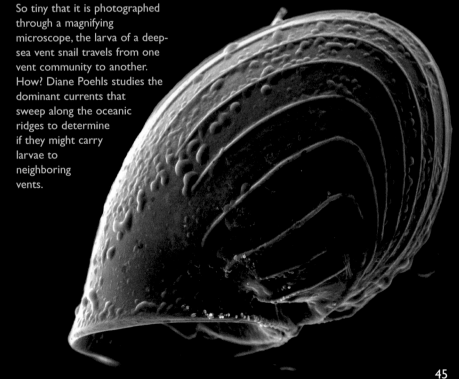

45

Going

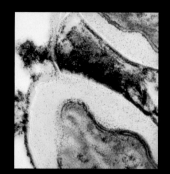

For years, scientists sounded like Goldilocks in the story of Goldilocks and the three bears as they looked for life in our solar system. Venus and Mercury were "too hot;" the outer planets and Mars were "too cold." Only Earth was "just right" — so perfect for supporting life, it's nicknamed the Goldilocks Zone.

Scientists believed that, even on Earth, living things could survive only within certain limits: no hotter than California's Death Valley (desert lizards), no colder than Antarctica (penguins), and no higher than commercial aircraft (bar-headed geese). In these pages you'll find animals who have s-s-s-s-s-stretched the Goldilocks Zone. Zoom in for a look — and turn the page.

Mars landscape

to X-tremes

Camels Worth Their Salt

The Lop Nur Gobi Desert in China is one of the most severe environments on Earth. Wild Bactrian camels have been forced into this harsh environment by the spread of human communities.

Although wild and domestic Bactrian camels look almost identical, local herdsmen can track the wild camels by following their distinctive footprints.

Pour salt into a glass of water and take a sip. Yuck! Like you, all mammals need fresh water to survive. Or do they?

Explorer John Hare believes it possible that the wild Bactrian (two-humped) camels that live in the "lost world" of the Lop Nur Gobi Desert in China's Xinjiang Province could be a new species. This remarkable animal survives the harsh environment by drinking the salt-water slush that bubbles up beneath the desert sand — water that its cousin, the domestic Bactrian camel will not touch.

What is it about the livers, kidneys, and lungs of these wild Bactrian camels that enables them to exist without fresh water? That's what scientists would like to know. Unfortunately, finding individual camels to study hasn't been easy. Talking with local herdsmen, scientists have determined that the population of wild Bactrian camels in China numbers a mere 600. A further 300 wild camels are believed to live in the Gobi Desert in Mongolia.

Twin Camels

The wild Bactrian camels look so much like their domesticated cousins that only people who spend a lot of time with camels can tell them apart. If you look very closely, you might see that the humps on the wild camel (left) are spaced farther apart, and are smaller and pointier, than those of the domestic Bactrian (right).

Are these camels really a new species? No one knows for sure yet, but early results from genetic testing look promising. Professor Han Jianlin, a molecular geneticist, found a 3% difference in the genetic makeup of wild and domestic camels. This may not sound like much — until you consider that there is a 2.3% difference between gorillas and chimpanzees.

Humans keep making life more and more dangerous for wild camels. The inhospitable desert they call home has been used for nuclear-weapons testing for almost 50 years. When testing stopped in the late 1990s, the area was opened to people. This introduced a new threat to the camels — poachers who hunt them for meat. John worked with the governments of China and Mongolia, and a number of international organizations, to establish the Lop Nur Wild Camel Reserve to protect the camels and their extreme habitat.

As of 2004, only 18 wild Bactrian camels lived in captivity. If they do turn out to be a new species, they will be more endangered than the rare giant panda.

John Hare

Ever since he was a small boy, John wanted to explore remote places. He fell in love with deserts and took many expeditions by camel into some of the remotest places on Earth. Today, John is determined to save the wild Bactrian camels, one of the rarest animals in the world. He is the founder of Wild Camel Protection Foundation and a member of the Explorers Club of America.

Recipes for Life

Take a deep breath. Sip some water. Let the sun warm your face. Oxygen, water, and sunlight are such a basic part of your world, you may not think of them as your life-support system. Without them, there would be no life — at least, not life as we usually think about it.

But for some new species, the basics of life are very different. In 1994, Danish scientists found a completely new kind of animal down a dark, cold-water well in Greenland. The new creature, *Limnognathia maerski*, feeds on bacteria and algae that it scrapes off underwater moss using its complicated jaws. This is only the fourth time in the last 100 years that scientists have discovered a species that does not fit any of the previously known animal families. In 2002, Belgian scientists also found this tiny beast on the subantarctic Crozet Islands.

All over the world, scientists are discovering new species thriving in impossible conditions. These "extremophiles" —

This new species, *Limnognathia maerski*, first found in Greenland, likes cold conditions so much, scientists are keeping a colony in a refrigerator. You could fit ten of these tiny creatures on a single hair.

Psychophiles love the cold so much, this scene would be like a tropical vacation for them. Some reproduce on the super-cold ocean floor.

Thermophiles crave temperatures way, way hotter than a tropical vacation. A few species have even been found to survive above 110°C (212°F) — that's hotter than the boiling temperature of water.

from the word *extreme* and *-phile*, which is Greek for "lover" — thrive in conditions that would kill humans in seconds flat. They demand such a different recipe for life, they don't fit any of the five kingdoms in Linnaean classification. Named *Archaea* (from the Greek word meaning "ancient"), these microscopic organisms are grouped by the mind-boggling conditions in which they live.

The thrilling discovery of life in entirely new ecosystems stretches the Goldilocks Zone wider and wider. If organisms can live without oxygen and sunlight under unbelievable pressures, temperatures, and caustic conditions here on Earth, where else might life be possible?

A for Archaea; B for Bacteria

Archaea look and act a lot like bacteria. In fact, when your parents were your age, scientists assumed archaea were a kind of weird bacteria. Recent genetic analysis reveals that the two groups are distinctly different, so Bacteria and Archaea have now been assigned to their own separate domains, different branches on the tree of life.

Halophiles are salt lovers — but to live in, not to sprinkle on food. Some species thrive in water ten times saltier than the sea.

Acidophiles prefer acidic conditions. Some species are found in the sulfurous gases in hydrothermal vents, or in conditions so acidic they would cause your skin to fall apart.

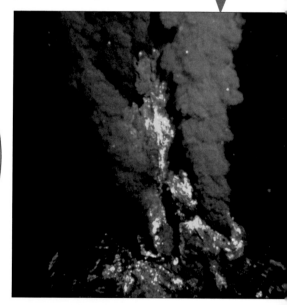

Chemical Alley

In 2003, a team of Mexican and American scientists discovered blobs of cracked asphalt at the bottom of the Gulf of Mexico. Traces of ancient, undersea alleys? The truth is even more amazing. They were created naturally when oil deposits, thrust upward by salt domes, caused tar to flow like lava. Miles beneath the ocean surface, scientists looked between the cracks in the asphalt . . . and discovered life. Microorganisms, mussels, tubeworms — an entire ecosystem flourishes in an underwater world without sunlight. As they do in deep-sea vents (see page 45), different species work together to create the energy they need to live.

X-treme SPF

Great Salt Lake, in the state of Utah, is almost ten times saltier than the sea. Life just shouldn't be able to exist here. But in 2004, Bonnie Baxter and her scientific colleagues determined that the lake is teeming with life. It is home to dozens of species of halophiles (salt-loving microbes) that thrive in salty water. They have microscopic solar-powered salt pumps that allow them to produce energy from sunlight. But in order to gather the solar energy to run their pumps, halophiles spend a lot of time basking in the sunlight at the water's surface. How do they safely endure such incredible levels of ultraviolet (UV) exposure?

Looking like bright beads, individual halophiles (above) produce color pigments. Thousands of colonies of halophiles contain thousands of cells, to give the Great Salt Lake a pinkish hue (left).

The Great Salt Lake of Utah in the US is the largest salt lake in the western hemisphere.

A Lo-o-o-ong Sleep

For some species, what is extreme is how long they live. Microorganisms have apparently survived for 4,800 years in the brickwork of Peruvian pyramids, and maybe even 300 million years in coal. Others have turned up alive in the 11,000-year-old gut of a well-preserved mastodon and the 30-million-year-old digestive tract of a bee trapped in amber. Amazingly, halophiles found in 250-million-year-old salt deposits have been brought back to life. It makes scientists wonder — could halophiles be sleeping in the ancient salt lake on Mars?

The answer is a colorful one. Pink, purple, orange — halophiles are full of color pigments called carotenoids. Bonnie is eager to learn why these carotenoids provide sun protection, and if carotenoids ingested by humans could have a similar effect. She hopes the secrets of these organisms can be used to prevent UV damage to humans in our increasingly sun-blasted world.

Almost nothing is known about these extraordinary organisms of the lake. Scientists don't know enough about the basic life requirements of most halophiles to grow them successfully. Scientists studying microbes compare the DNA of a new species to an existing gene bank of known organisms, and normally they find matches three out of four times. But when Bonnie and her colleagues do this with the new species from Great Salt Lake, they almost never find a match. Halophiles are unlike anything else on Earth!

RESEARCHER PROFILE

Bonnie Baxter

Bonnie has been interested in science for as long as she can remember. Her dad jokes that when other kids were bringing home story-books from the library, Bonnie was checking out books on electromagnetism. Bonnie believes children are naturally keen on science and she credits her parents and teachers for nurturing her passion. She dedicated her Ph.D. in their honor. Today she is an associate professor of biology at Westminster College in Utah.

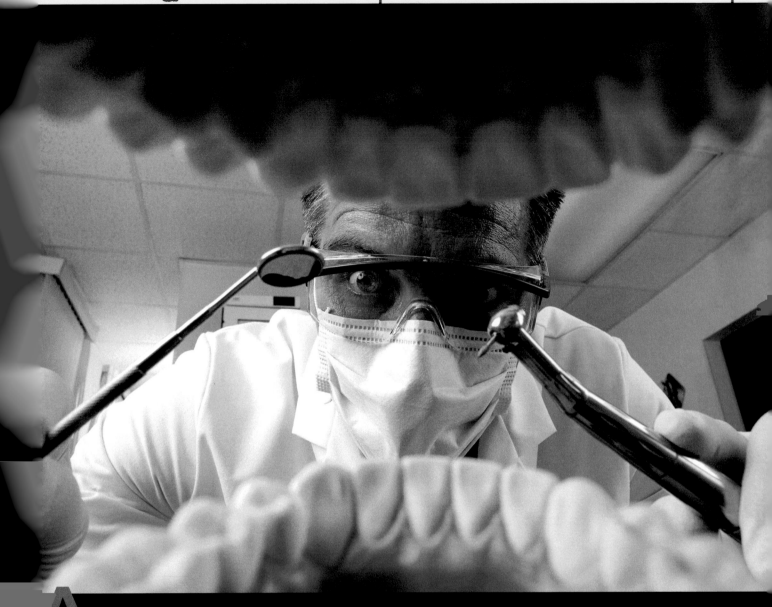

Apart from any jitters you might feel when you're sitting there, what's so extreme about a dentist's chair? The answer is bacteria.

Bacteria are living organisms, but it's almost impossible for us to relate to their lives. Imagine a whole lifetime that can be as short as 15 minutes. Think about living entirely in a space less than a thousandth the thickness of an eyelash. What would it be like if day or night, weather, and up or down were meaningless? Bacteria live in every place you can imagine — in the clouds, on an Antarctic ice floe, at the bottom of the sea, in a rotting peach, in solid rock below the surface of the Earth, on this book, and even in the chewing

. in Your Mouth

Dental plaque is made up of food remains and more than 500 species of densely packed bacteria. The bacteria in the plaque feed on the sugars in the food particles and produce acid. Because this acid causes tooth decay, dentists are eager to find out how the bacteria work together to attach to the enamel of your teeth. Recent research suggests that the first bacteria to settle on a tooth weave tiny microbial mats that form the support structures upon which other species of bacteria can grow.

With everything advertised as "antibacterial" these days, it's no secret that bacteria can make you sick. If you've ever had an ear infection or strep throat, your doctor probably prescribed an antibiotic medicine to kill the bacteria causing the infection. Unfortunately, bacteria reproduce and change so quickly that some of them develop resistance to the drug. So it makes sense that one of the best places to study the development of new species is in a crowded hospital, where bacteria rapidly reproduce and build up resistance to existing drugs.

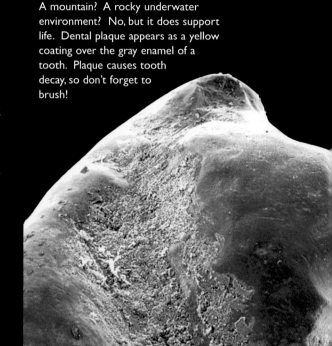

A mountain? A rocky underwater environment? No, but it does support life. Dental plaque appears as a yellow coating over the gray enamel of a tooth. Plaque causes tooth decay, so don't forget to brush!

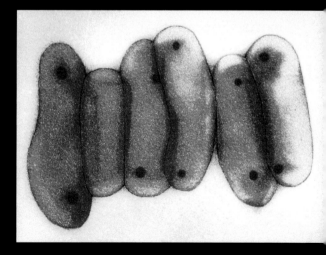

They may look pretty here, but these are the bacteria that cause the lung disease tuberculosis: the original strain (above) changed to become resistant to antibiotics (left). The images have been magnified and colored, so it's easy to see that new species are developing before our eyes. Unless we take antibiotics properly, doctors worry that bacteria will develop resistance faster than scientists are able to develop new antibiotics.

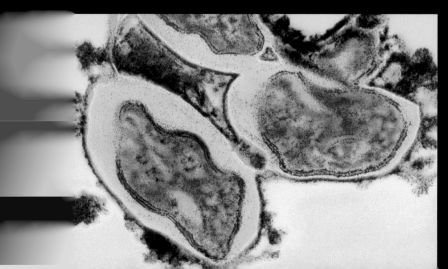

Tiny Ecosystems

What do astrobiology (the study of life in the universe) and dentistry have in common? The answer is microbial mats. It turns out that microbial mats, just like the ones bacteria weave to create dental plaque (see page 55), are the Earth's oldest known ecosystems. Fossil evidence dates them at 3.4 billion years of age. In fact, microorganisms (also called microbes) were the only form of life for more than 80% of the entire history of life on Earth.

Microbial mats may be able to tell us how life got started on our planet. Kelly Decker, a soil scientist working with the National Aeronautic and Space Administration (NASA), studies places on Earth where little oxygen exists. She wants to learn about ancient microbial ecosystems — how they formed, and how they were able to take in sunlight and produce the oxygen atmosphere we enjoy on Earth today. Astrobiologists hope to use the models developed by these studies to scan far-away planets for distant signs of life.

Green, purple, green . . . this colorful microbial mat from Mexico (top) shows a classic pattern made by different species of bacteria. You see brilliant colors in Manitoba, Canada, too. Stained by iron, the green algae that make up most of this microbial mat (bottom) appear vivid orange.

RESEARCHER PROFILE

Kelly Decker

There was never a question in Kelly's mind that she would grow up to become a scientist. As a child she spent many hours looking in dark places to find life. She learned that ecology isn't always showy like a rain forest, but can occur under rotting logs and leaves at the base of a redwood, or in the seawalls on the coast. In school, she learned to appreciate the processes ecosystems use to live and breathe. She continues to study these processes where she finds them. Kelly is a research scientist at the NASA-Ames Research Center.

Look Very Closely

If you really want to find a new species, think small. Kathleen Londry (above), a University of Manitoba astrobiologist, says there's so much diversity in the microbial world, it makes the combined diversity of every animal species seem like a drop in a lake by comparison. Even though thousands of species of bacteria have been isolated, scientists believe there are at least tens of thousands and probably millions of species of microbes yet to be discovered.

No, it's not art — it's not even made by humans. Scrape away the top layer of sand from a Massachusetts' salt marsh and you'll discover microbial mats in the shape of purple rainbows.

Called stromatolites, these strange underwater structures are formed when microbial mats develop slowly and trap sand. Fossil stromatolites are the oldest record of life on Earth.

HOT DEBATE ARE MICROBES IN CHINA AND CANADA THE SAME?

New research suggests that many species of microbes can be found only in specific locations. If this is true, then the microscopic world of species might be as diverse as the larger world of plants and animals that we can see. That would mean that the total number of microorganisms in the world — and therefore the total number of all species in the world — is much higher than previously estimated. But Kathleen Londry thinks these findings are probably an exception to the more common rule that "everything is everywhere." So, she argues, although the microbes in your water glass are quite different from the microbes on the table it is sitting on, they

Microbial
Life on Mars?

Although Mars is now a desolate desert, a host of clues remain
from an earlier era, billions of years ago, hinting that the Red
Planet was once host to great rivers, lakes, and perhaps even an
ocean. The designated landing site for the first Mars Exploration
Rover mission, Gusev Crater on Mars was formed by a
meteorite impact.

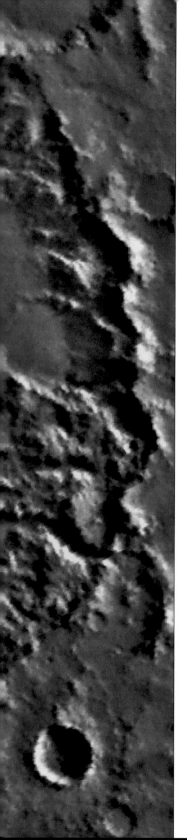

While some astrobiologists send rovers into space to search for extraterrestrial life, others stay closer to home, studying microbes found in Earth's extreme places to better understand how life might exist in other parts of our solar system. All life needs water, and mounting evidence suggests that Mars may once have been a very wet place.

As the conditions on early Mars got harsher, it lost liquid water through evaporation. Remaining bodies of water would have been increasingly salty places. Take Gusev Crater. If water was present on Mars when it was formed 3.5 billion years ago, as some researchers believe, it would have flowed into Gusev Crater through channels in a huge canyon. Because the crater has no outlet, water could not flow out. It would have developed a high concentration of salts and minerals.

Mono Lake in northern California is undergoing a very similar process today. Water flows in from streams, but there's no way out again except evaporation — a process that constantly increases the concentration of salts and minerals. In 2003, astrobiologists probing the oxygen-deprived mud of Mono Lake made a startling discovery — a new species of microbe called *Spirochaeta americana* was found in this Mars-like environment!

Photographed here from space, Mono Lake is a volcanic basin at the north end of Long Valley Caldera, one of North America's most active regions for earthquakes and volcanoes.

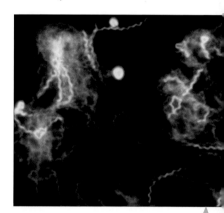

Spirochaeta americana is a new species that grows without oxygen in the highly acidic and super-salty conditions of Mono Lake.

Moon Monsters?

Two of Jupiter's moons — Ganymede and Europa — may also have supported large bodies of water, making them good candidates for extraterrestrial life.

HOT DEBATE ARE THERE NEW SPECIES ON MARS?

When astrobiologists debate the possibility of life on Mars, they usually end up talking about water. Without water, there can be no life as we know it. If, as some scientists argue, it has been 3.5 billion years since liquid water was present on Mars, then the chance of finding life there is remote. But if water is present on Mars now as others claim, then

Tiptoe through the collections area of a natural history museum and you'll uncover unbelievable treasures — dinosaur bones in plaster jackets, cabinets filled with bird feathers, whale skeletons several shelves long, cartons packed with jars of worms! Each specimen tells a story that reaches back millions of years into the past, a story that enables scientists to piece together the extraordinary diversity of species on Earth. Can modern science create "new" species from the bones, fur, feathers, and scales from some of these long dead creatures? Prepare to be amazed . . . and turn the page.

Bird collection at the National Museum of Natural History, Washington, D.C.

Not Forgotten

Bones Tell a Story

In 2001, scientists at the Royal Ontario Museum in Canada and at Oxford University, England, became the first to identify the complete DNA sequence of an extinct animal — the moa — from its bones. What can the bones of an extinct moa tell scientists about today's species of flightless birds? Plenty!

The new information is causing ornithologists to look at the family tree of flightless birds in new ways. The extinct New Zealand moa has traditionally been lumped together with the living New Zealand kiwi, because they look somewhat alike. But genetic analysis reveals that the kiwi is more closely related to the Australian cassowary and emu. The more scientists know about classifying species of birds, the better they can identify a new species when it is found.

Studying old species can also tell us which of them are "new" or separate species. Female moas differ genetically from the male birds, so DNA analysis reveals which remains are from she-birds and which are from he-birds. It turns out that female moas were larger than males, and that scientists in the past who had classified the "big" and "little" ones as different species were incorrect.

Moas were a group of large flightless birds that lived in New Zealand until they were hunted to extinction 400 years ago. This reproduction of a stout-legged moa shows that these birds resembled today's flightless birds.

DNA is rarely preserved in fossils, because it breaks down easily under heat, water, and other forces. Luckily, the bones of moas, like this skeleton, can be found in alpine caves where the cold temperatures and shelter from the elements have protected the DNA.

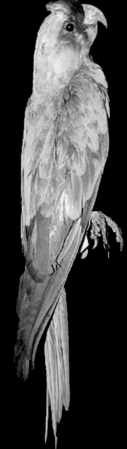

When you see brightly colored birds, you might think of the tropics. But the Carolina Parakeet *Conuropsis carolinensis* flew wild in North America until it disappeared in the 1920s. Scientists have started to perform DNA analysis on samples of toe muscle, taken from old museum specimens like this one, to try to determine the closest living relatives of the Carolina Parakeet.

What's Up, Doc?

Recently, scientists shopping in a market in Laos made a remarkable discovery — a black-and-brown striped bunny with a red rump. The only other striped rabbit in the world is the highly endangered Sumatran Rabbit (below). Except for this picture taken with a "photo trap" (a camera with a motion sensor), the Sumatran Rabbit hasn't been seen since 1916. By comparing DNA from the newly discovered bunny with DNA from Sumatran Rabbits that have spent 100 years in a British museum collection, scientists confirmed that the newly named annamite rabbit is indeed a new species.

Say Goodbye!

New species have been appearing and disappearing ever since life first appeared on our planet. According to Stephen Jay Gould, the noted paleontologist, 99% of all the plant and animal species that have ever existed have already become extinct, many leaving no trace of their existence in the fossil record.

Whale of a Tale

They swim free in the ocean, instead of lying extinct in a museum collection, but many types of whales are rare. Study of live whales combined with genetic analysis of specimens is the best way to find new species of these massive sea mammals.

Killer whales — *orcinus orca* — in British Columbia, Canada, provide an exciting example of how some new species evolve. The British Columbia coast is home to at least two distinct killer whale "races" or "cultures." Resident killer whales eat only fish. Transient killer whales eat only seals, sea lions, and other marine mammals. They use different calls, or "dialects," to allow members of each pod to learn from and identify with each other.

Extra-Large New Species

Believe it or not, discoveries of enormous new species still happen today. In 2003, Japanese researchers announced the discovery of a new species of whale. *Balaenoptera omurai* belongs to a group of whales called rorquals, and is the length of two school buses. Surprisingly, the true identity of these giant beasts was hidden in skeletons stored in the collections area of the National Science Museum in Tokyo for 25 years. The skeletons of these mystery whales were donated by whalers in the late 1970s. When a similar whale carcass washed ashore in the Sea of Japan in 1998, scientists compared DNA samples from it with those of the museum specimens, leading to their extraordinary discovery.

Although they live in the same waters off the BC coast, transient (above) and resident (below) killer whales live in separate cultures, and are becoming increasingly different.

When rare whales are caught, it can send scientists back to the museum. This whale, on board the Japanese whaling ship that transported the whale skeletons stored in the National Science Museum in Tokyo, was caught in the Solomon Sea in 1976.

HOT DEBATE — KILLER WHALES — ONE SPECIES OR TWO?

Resident and transient killer whales do not interbreed, even though they swim in the same areas of the Pacific Ocean. DNA tests show consistent genetic differences between the two types. As long as they stick to their own traditions and their different menu, the gap between transient and resident killer whales will widen. Scientist Lance Barrett-Lennard believes they are in the process of developing into separate species. Other scientists argue that they are already separate species, and that each of these smaller species groups should be given conservation protection under the US Endangered Species Act.

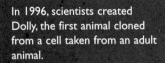

In 1996, scientists created Dolly, the first animal cloned from a cell taken from an adult animal.

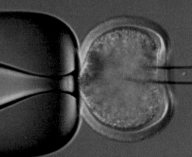

Cloning involves a complicated series of procedures, in which scientists transfer DNA from one animal into the cells of another.

Place a picture face down on a copy machine and press Start. Faster than you can say "the clone zone," you have an identical copy. Cloning is a process that produces identical copies too, but with a big difference — the copies are alive! A clone is a genetically identical copy of another living organism.

Not surprisingly, making a clone is a whole lot trickier than producing a photocopy. In the case of Dolly the sheep, scientists put genetic material in a mammal egg that had been specially prepared. The egg was then placed in the uterus of an adult female sheep, where it continued to develop until birth.

Using a different technique, European scientists produced the first surviving clone of an endangered animal, a wild sheep called a mouflon, in 2001. A year later, American scientists announced that they had cloned the first pet — a calico kitten.

So cloning works — Jurassic Park, here we come! But is it really possible to clone a Tyrannosaurus rex? Many paleontologists (scientists who study ancient life) don't think so, because DNA breaks down over time when exposed to air or water, or when it is frozen and thawed. The oldest authenticated DNA comes from plants that lived in Siberia 400,000 years ago, but that's incredibly young compared to a 65 million year old dinosaur.

The final word on cloning belongs to nature. Not all clones are produced by people. Cloning is the most natural thing in the world — for bacteria and for some species of animals, such as snails and shrimp. The species of shrimp *Artemia perthenogenetica* has been reproducing itself by cloning for at least 30 million years.

Although cc was born December 22, 2001, the scientists who created her delayed the announcement of her cloning until her immune system was fully developed — and she had all the shots you get for your pet cat.

The first kitty ever cloned was named "cc" — the old abbreviation for "carbon copy," and also the acronym for "copy cat." It is shown here (left) at seven weeks old. The fully grown cat (above left) is Rainbow, cc's genetic donor. Surprisingly, the two don't look identical, because the pattern on a cat's coat is only partly determined by genetics — pre-birth conditions, such as temperature in the mother's womb, may also affect a cat's color.

Back to Life

This painting shows the now extinct Tasmanian tiger. They looked like large, long dogs with heavy, stiff tails and big heads.

We all know that when an animal goes extinct, it is lost forever. Well, a team of scientists working in Australia is challenging that belief by attempting to clone an old favorite from the past. If they are successful, the Tasmanian tiger *Thylacinus cynocephalus* may roam the island of Tasmania decades after becoming extinct.

You probably wouldn't recognize a Tasmanian tiger — or thylacine — unless you came across a stuffed specimen in a museum. These night-roving, meat-eating marsupials with the tiger-striped backs were unlike any mammal living today. Tasmanian tigers were found in Australia for at least 12 million years, disappearing from the mainland about 3,000 years ago when the dingo (related to the domestic dog) was introduced. They continued to thrive on the dingo-free island of Tasmania, until they were eventually wiped out by hunters, sheep ranchers, and disease.

So how do you get Tasmanian tiger babies if there are no parents left to produce them? For Don Colgan, head of the Australian Museum's department of evolutionary biology, finding the answer started with a baby Tasmanian tiger — or joey. The joey was

A Tasmanian tiger in captivity in 1922. The last one died in an Australian zoo in 1936.

HOT DEBATE   IS CLONING ANIMALS GOOD OR BAD?

Re-creating an extinct species is so challenging it may never happen. But the cloning of Dolly the sheep in 1996 sparked the dream of re-creating favorite species from the past and present. Some people feel that trying to clone very rare or endangered species might be a necessary way to prevent them from going extinct. They argue that for many rare animals reluctant to breed in captivity, such as giant pandas, cloning could be a way to create new individuals. Other people believe that trying to clone any species is tampering with nature and should never be attempted. Cloning raises tough questions about what is good and bad or right and wrong. Do you like to debate these sorts of issues? Maybe you're a natural-born bio-ethicist — a person who studies collected from its mother's pouch in 1866 (when it was between four and six months old) and preserved in a jar of ethanol at the museum. Strands of DNA collected from the baby were in surprisingly good condition for such an old specimen, and Colgan hoped that they would serve as the starting point from which future tigers could be cloned.

But it was too good to be true. The DNA turned out to be contaminated with DNA from other species, mostly human and algae. In 2001, scientists extracted DNA from a bone and a tooth from two adult thylacines found in the museum's collections. The following year, they used it to replicate some of the Tasmanian tiger's genes. They were excited to find that the "dead" DNA reacted the way live DNA does. And the DNA was not contaminated. One step closer to the goal.

The chances of successfully cloning a Tasmanian tiger are small. It took 276 tries to produce Dolly the sheep, and it's many times more difficult with extinct animals.

Researchers from France, Japan, and the US have collected DNA from frozen woolly mammoths in Siberia and Alaska, in the hopes of re-creating a species that lived 100,000 years ago. So far, the strands of DNA they have collected are too fragmented to be used effectively. ▼

R E S E A R C H E R   P R O F I L E

Don Colgan

Don Colgan can still remember the first time he saw the whale skeleton hanging in the lobby of the Australian Museum. It was an exciting experience for the eight-year-old boy who spent happy days exploring the biology of the dry, red creek beds lined with eucalyptus trees near his hometown of Broken Hill. Today, Don is the principal research scientist in the Evolutionary Biology Unit of the Australian Museum.

Ages Old

Five to ten million years — that's the average age of all the plant and animal species that can be seen without the aid of a microscope. Scientists often estimate the ages of species by comparing fossils found in rock layers dating from different ages. Most of these new species appeared and disappeared long before humans evolved on Earth. However, some fascinating species lived then ... and are still going strong! Today, scientists use fossil evidence and DNA analysis to try to get the scoop on the world's oldest birthdays.

Leaves from gingko trees, like this one above, look so much like the fossilized leaf imprints in rock that's 135–210 million years old, the trees have been nicknamed "living fossils."

A fossilized leaf from a gingko tree.

Many newly discovered species have actually been around for a very long time. In 2003, scientists working in the Western Ghat Mountains of southern India announced that they had found a bright purple pig-nosed frog. *Nasikabatrachus sahyadrensis* is the first discovery of a new species, genus, and scientific family of frogs since 1926. And it has a fascinating history ... or, make that prehistory. Researchers say the tiny-headed amphibian descended from a frog that hopped around the feet of dinosaurs 130 million years ago.

No fossils from this type of frog exist. What clues helped scientists to determine the age of the pig-nosed frog's ancestors? They compared DNA from this frog with that of many other frog species, including one living in the Seychelles in the Indian Ocean. The results confirmed that the two frogs are distant relatives, probably linked by a common ancestor that once lived on the supercontinent Pangaea. One hundred million years ago, Pangaea broke apart, roughly forming the continents we know today. The frogs in the Seychelles evolved into one species; those in India became another.

It is not surprising that this new species *Nasikabatrachus sahyadrensis* went undetected for so long. Pig-nosed frogs spend 50 weeks of each year underground in their burrows, emerging at the beginning of the monsoon season to breed.

Don't Swat That Fly!

You are looking at a species that first appeared in its present form 35 to 40 million years ago, as this fossil demonstrates. Insects, as a group of species, are very ancient inhabitants of the Earth, almost twice as old as the reptiles and two-and-a-half times as old as the mammals — perhaps seven times as old as hominids, the mammalian group that you belong to.

Same Old

Tropical rain forests are very old living ecosystems. Fossil records show that the forests of Southeast Asia haven't changed much since the time when horned dinosaurs wandered through them — between 70 and 100 million years ago!

Species Senior Citizens

- 395,000 years: age of the oldest fragments of DNA recovered so far, collected from Siberian and Alaskan permafrost

- 6 million years: age of sandhill crane *Grus canadensis*, one of the oldest surviving species of birds

- 300 million years: length of time paddlefish *Polydon spathula* have existed virtually unchanged in North America

- 400 million years: estimated age of chimaera, the oldest group of fish species alive today

On the Fast Track

Some Galapagos land snails are skinny (see *Bulimulus reibischi* below bottom) while others are round (see *Bulimulus ochsneri* below top). Biologist Christine Parent thinks the shape of the skinny shell, with a small opening, means less moisture loss in dry climates, and she has indeed found this kind of snail in the driest habitats.

▼

What's faster, a horse or a snail? For many years, scientists thought that horses had one of the fastest records of speciation (development of new species). But a new study suggests that land snails may have had just as fast, if not faster, evolutionary horsepower.

The Galapagos Islands that Charles Darwin found so intriguing are home to an explosion of land snail diversity. Whereas an impressive 20 to 40 species live in mainland South America, a whopping 65 species are found on one or another of the ten major islands in the Galapagos Archipelago.

How quickly do new species of snails evolve? Tracing back through the geological record of the islands' volcanic rocks, and piecing together a family tree based on the DNA relationships between the snails, biologist Christine Parent has determined that more than one new land snail species appears each million years. That might sound even slower than snails slime their way around, but it's downright speedy in evolutionary terms.

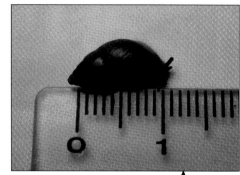

This land snail has not yet been identified. Not only is it tiny — the ruler is marked in centimetres (1 cm = 0.4 in.) — but it is probably a very young species, as it is found on one of the youngest of the Galapagos Islands.

R E S E A R C H E R   P R O F I L E

Christine Parent

Christine was always very curious as a child, and she loved to explore the wild areas around her family home in Quebec. She was keen on insects but not fond of slugs — ironic, given her current devotion to snails, animals she calls "those cute slugs with little houses." Christine decided to be a scientist when she visited the Galapagos Islands at the age of 17. Today, she is finishing her Ph.D. at Simon Fraser University.

Scientists walk in the limestone cave on the island of Flores in Indonesia where *Homo floresiensis* was discovered.

The skull and bones of Flores Woman (shown here displayed in Jakarta) were easier to excavate than the other skeletons. The bones of the other eight *Homo floresiensis* bodies were not fossilized, as their age and the dampness of the cave where they were found had given them a texture like mashed potatoes.

Our ancient relatives share the genus Homo with us, but scientists believed that they lived too long ago to share the Earth with us. But in 2004, a group of Indonesian researchers on the island of Flores made an astonishing discovery — a new species of tiny, human-like "hobbits" they've named *Homo floresiensis*. These amazing little people stood just a metre (3 ft.) tall. They made tools, hunted (and probably cooked) elephants the size of Shetland ponies, and lived just 18,000 years ago.

Flores Woman (as the most complete skeleton has been nicknamed) was perfectly proportioned, with a skull no bigger than a grapefruit. The most likely theory is that her species evolved from *Homo erectus* (one of those older human species). Perhaps some of her ancestors reached Flores by raft. Over generations, they became smaller and smaller — just as the tiny elephants whose bones were found in the cave along with the new "human" species did.

One Fish, Two Fish ... Many, Many Fish

Lake Victoria in East Africa is home to between 300 and 500 species of fish called cichlids. Every one of these species came from a single ancestor. Using geological techniques, some scientists have determined that the lake was totally dry 12,000 years ago. If they are correct, that single species of cichlid may have given rise to hundreds of new species within just 12,000 years!

HOT DEBATE WE ARE THE ONLY HUMANS ... OR ARE WE?

Of the millions of species on Earth, only one species is human. But *Homo floresiensis* seems to have been quite human, a lot like us. How much alike? Leading scientists from Indonesia, Australia, Britain, and other countries believe that *Homo floresiensis* is not a member of our species. The discovery of Flores Woman suggests that until very recently we *Homo sapiens* were not alone, but shared the world with people of another species. Researchers are hopeful that they might find DNA in the bones that will help to determine where *Homo floresiensis* fits into the human family tree.

Surprises in

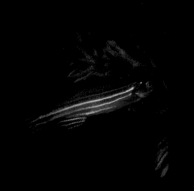

Take a walk in the park, and roll down a grassy hillside. Take a dip in a pool. Gaze at the creatures in a local pet shop. Open a kitchen cupboard and look for a snack. Believe it or not, these are just a few of the everyday places where people have discovered new species. Even the most familiar life form could be a new species — you just have to look at it the right way. Your everyday environment could be home to an exotic collection of strange new life, from ancient amphibians to surprising new foods. Eager to find new species close to home? Turn the page!

Central Park, New York

Everyday Life

How Bison Make Sunflowers

Ever planted sunflower seeds as a class project? These hardy plants love dry, disturbed soil so much that they can grow taller than you, even if you forget to water them. When Loren Rieseberg thinks of sunflowers, he imagines long trails of bright yellow petals stretching as far as the eye can see.

As an evolutionary biologist, Loren is interested in how new species form, and sunflowers have provided him with some remarkable clues. Two species of sunflowers flourished in the Great American Plains thousands of years ago. When bison arrived on the scene, their travels caused pollen and seeds from the common sunflower and the petioled sunflower to mix with one another. The new hybrid (result of breeding two species) was the anomalous sunflower.

Loren and his students were eager to learn how long it took the new species of sunflower to form in the wild. They recreated the sequence of events in a greenhouse — bringing together the two species of sunflower as the bison did. Loren assumed that he could interbreed two different species of sunflower to get another species. What he didn't know was how long it might take, and if he would get the anomalous sunflower or a totally different species. He was amazed to find that the anomalous sunflower species evolved in just four generations. That means that, in the wild, the new species could have developed in as little as 60 years. Loren believes that future experiments will support this remarkable finding — that evolution is much more repeatable and predictable than anyone had thought.

Against the backdrop of the North American Great Plains, the evolution of the new hybrid anomalous sunflower involved a beautiful setting, magnificent bison — and time. ▼

Herds of wild bison *(Bison bison)* crisscrossed the Great Plains of North America dating back 200,000 years. The wear and tear of millions and millions of hooves plowed trenches so deep, only the bison's woolly heads could be seen. As bison walked, the sunflower seeds tangled into their fur dropped into the broken-up soil beneath their feet, leaving one of the world's largest sunflower gardens in their wake.

Long ago, they shared a common ancestor, but the common sunflower *Helianthus annuus* (left) and the petioled sunflower *Helianthus petiolaris* (right) were separated by geography and evolved into different species. This is the most common way species are formed.

In all of Loren's greenhouse trials, the anomalous sunflower *(Helianthus anomalus)* shown in this photo below appeared within four generations.

RESEARCHER PROFILE

Loren Rieseberg

Loren grew up in a country home and always loved the outdoors. His passion for studying plants was inspired when he took a wilderness survival camping trip in Canada and discovered the fun of identifying and feasting on wild edible plants. Loren is a distinguished professor of biology at Indiana University.

Old Familiar Places

When the sun shines down on a hot summer's day, the lucky citizens of Austin, Texas, can take a refreshing swim in Barton Springs pool. The pool is fed from underground springs and the water is refreshingly chilly all year round. People have been swimming here for more than 100 years, and it turns out they had unexpected company.

Barton Springs pool is the only place in the world where you can find *Eurycea sosorum,* the Barton Springs salamander. People were so excited to discover this new species in the early 1990s that they set up a weekly volunteer diving survey to monitor the health of the salamanders. Scientists studied them, biology students earned graduate degrees describing what they ate and how they lived, and the US government even granted the little creatures endangered species protection. And then, in 2001, another new species of salamander was identified in the pool!

The Barton Springs salamander is small enough to fit in your hand. This lungless amphibian spends all its life in the water, breathing through a pair of red gills located behind its head. ▼

▲ The discovery of the Austin blind salamander in an Austin pool proves that you don't need to travel to the bottom of the ocean or the top of a tropical rain forest to find a new species.

When the Austin blind salamander *Eurycea waterlooensis* is young, it looks a lot like the Barton Springs salamander. It was only after scientists began a captive-breeding program for Barton Springs salamanders that they discovered that some of the juveniles turned into these different-looking adults. One of the scientists who worked to make the identification is herpetologist (scientist who studies amphibians and reptiles) David Hillis. David is thrilled that another new species turned up in a popular swimming pool in the heart of a busy city. It supports his belief that great discoveries are just waiting to be made all around, as long as you are open and curious about the creatures that live in your very own neighborhood.

Perfectly Wizardly

What could be more everyday than your favorite book? Botanist Lena Stuwe and her colleague Jason Grant were driving through misty mountains and lush vegetation in Ecuador when they spotted a strange plant growing by the roadside. Without any flowers, the plant was impossible to identify as a new species, so they started to search for a flowering one. Hours later, as darkness approached, they were rain-soaked and ready to give up. And that's when a tall flowering plant magically appeared before them. It stood as tall as a tree and was dripping with yellowish-white, bell-shaped flowers adapted for night pollination by bats and moths. In honor of the Harry Potter books, they named the new species of jungle plant *Macrocarpaea apparata* — "to apparate" is a wizard's ability to disappear and reappear somewhere else instantaneously.

David Hillis

David didn't have toys to play with when he was little. Instead, he played with the jungle animals he collected near his home in the Democratic Republic of the Congo in Africa (then called the Belgian Congo). Butterflies, lizards, snakes — David fell in love with the diversity of species he discovered in the jungle, and his enthusiasm for studying life has never stopped. Today he is a professor of integrative biology at the University of Texas at Austin

HOT DEBATE   HOW MANY PLANT SPECIES ARE AT RISK?

Even if you live in the heart of a city, there are plants all around you, but many plant species are at risk. How many? Depending on the type of evidence scientists use to estimate the total number of plant species, either too many — or much too many. According to the World Conservation Union (the world's largest association of scientists, governments, and nature-based organizations) 13% of the world's plant species are under threat. Recent research by two botanists from the US, however, argues that the number is really much greater — at least 22% and perhaps as high as 47%!

From Lab to Table

Corn with built-in insecticide. Rice enriched with vitamin A. Decaffeinated coffee beans straight from the plant. Today's news is full of amazing stories about the future of high-tech foods. Many of them are genetically modified organisms (GMOs) — plants, animals, or micro-organisms whose genetic material (DNA) has been altered in order to give them characteristics they don't have naturally.

Are GMOs new species? Some scientists say no, because many of these animals and plants can still reproduce with their "natural" relatives, which they could do only if they remained the same species. Other scientists say that some GMOs are new species based on their unique genetic makeups. No matter how you slice it, GM (genetically modified) plants and animals can be different from any other species naturally living on Earth.

In 1994, there were no GM crops grown commercially on farms anywhere in the world. Today, nearly one-quarter of all the world's crops are GM varieties. And scientists worldwide are cooking up surprising new ideas for the table. The US Department of Agriculture has more than 7,500 field tests on genetically modified foods currently underway.

A lab technician checks on futuristic peach and apple "orchards" (above). Each dish holds tiny experimental trees grown from lab-cultured cells to which researchers have given new genes. Will your foods be coming to your supermarket shelves from a traditional farm (top left) or from the lab in the future?

How many GM products are on the supermarket shelves already? GM ingredients are found in breads, cheeses, and sodas. Farmers have been raising GM food crops such as corn, soybeans, and canola since the mid-1990s. While you'll find few GM fruits or vegetables in your supermarket today, about 60% of highly processed foods like breakfast cereals contain some oils from GM corn, soy, or canola.

Cucaloupe ... or Melumber?

A team of American and Chinese scientists have created a new species from a cucumber and a cantaloupe melon. Crossbreeding different species of plants that live together in the same environment is nothing new. Farmers have been doing it for ages. That delicious Jonagold apple you buy at the market is a cross between the Jonathan apple and the Golden Delicious. What makes the cucaloupe (or do you prefer melumber?) different is that it was created through genetic engineering. Genetic engineering allows scientists to transfer genes between organisms that otherwise could not breed. The scientists involved in the study hope to use the new cross to breed cucumbers and melons that can resist disease.

'Za with the World

Scientists are testing GM varieties for many ingredients of everyone's favorite — pizza!

- Cheese: scientists genetically modify microorganisms involved in the cheese-making process to speed it up.
- Crust: wheat used in bleached flour can be genetically modified to make it easier to digest and less allergenic.
- Toppings: pineapples, green peppers, onions, and tomatoes can be genetically modified to stay fresh longer in supermarkets, resist pests, and survive droughts.

Medicine with more ap-peel!

Dislike needles? Hate taking pills? Bananas may soon offer an alternative. Scientists are experimenting with GM bananas and potatoes to create edible vaccines. The crops contain genetic material from harmful viruses — such as polio, cholera, and malaria — that would increase your immunity to sickness when you eat them.

Take the Taste Test

Do you like mustard on your hot dogs? Love to eat broccoli? When your grandparents were kids, a Danish botanist named Rolf Dahlgren noticed that people who liked mustard also tended to like the taste of brussels sprouts (below left), broccoli (below middle), and even nasturtium flowers (below right). Nasturtium, broccoli, mustard, and cabbage plants look quite different, but he believed they should be grouped together in the same scientific order. He reasoned that chemical compounds that some of us find tasty must be something they all had in common. Most scientists laughed at Dahlgren's idea, and eventually he gave up on his theory. Too bad he did. Recent DNA tests, used to classify plant species, confirm that Dahlgren was correct — these different-looking plants share a common genetic makeup.

HOT DEBATE ARE GMOS SAFE?

GM crops are approved by official food safety authorities, including Health Canada and the US Food and Drug Administration. Supporters praise GMO benefits like better nutrition, increased shelf-life, and reduced use of pesticides. But not everyone is convinced. All around the world, people are debating the possible dangers of GMOs to humans and the environment. Many scientists, like Alan McHughen, are involved in trying to bring scientific understanding to this debate. Alan writes books and gives speeches that help non-scientists understand the environmental and health impacts of both modern and traditional methods of food production. Check your library or search the Web for more on the pros and cons in this sizzling hot topic.

Pet Projects

These GloFish® are less than 3 centimetres (1 in.) long. Their bright red markings glow under black, fluorescent, or halogen lights.

Everything is quiet as you snuggle into bed. No fear of the dark for you. Thanks to your new pet GloFish®, you have company and a living night-light! GloFish® is the world's first genetically engineered or "transgenic" pet.

A transgenic species is an organism that has had part of another species' genetic code transferred into it. Surprisingly, GloFish® didn't start out as a trendy pet. GloFish® were developed in Singapore as a means to monitor water pollution. Researchers took a gene from coral that causes it to glow in polluted waters, and transferred it into the *Zebra danios* fish, hoping the fish would clue them in to the health of the water they put them in. But GloFish® glowed nonstop, whatever the state of the water they swam in!

And fish aren't the only transgenic pets that might be sharing your home in the near future. Scientists working with a company in the US called Transgenic Pets announced that they are trying to produce GM cats that will not cause allergic reactions. The sneezing, sore eyes, rashes, and asthma experienced by people with cat allergies are caused by a protein in the cat's skin and saliva. The researchers aim to take cat cells and knock out the gene's ability to produce the problem protein. The cell will be used to create an embryo that can be implanted into a surrogate mother cat that will give birth to a non-allergenic kitten.

There is *lots* of debate about whether creating genetically modified pets is a good idea. Some people are concerned about the potential impact of escaped GloFish® on wild fish populations. Others say the fish are perfectly safe. Some US states, like California, have banned their sale. Others, like Florida, have not. You can't buy them in Canada. What's your opinion?

Maybe you don't keep pets, but what about houseplants? Take the ideal Christmas tree — US researchers in Maine are working with tree growers to develop genetically modified evergreens that are perfectly shaped, disease-resistant, and faster growing. And with the help of an Australian company, a GM variety of purple — yes, purple! — carnations may soon be sitting on your table.

Science Fiction or Fact?

The AquAdvantage™ salmon (shown below the ruler) is four to six times larger than standard Atlantic salmon of the same age (shown above the ruler).

Ever thought about what it would be like to grow quickly? Really, really quickly? Scientists at Aqua Bounty Farms in Prince Edward Island, Canada, have some exciting news for you. By injecting growth-hormone genes into fertilized salmon eggs, they've genetically engineered salmon that reach full size four times faster than it would normally take.

But you won't find these transgenic super salmon on the barbecue just yet. Many scientists and environmental organizations are concerned that GM salmon will escape from farms and devastate populations of wild salmon. Because these GM fish grow faster,

The Genome Generation

Tweens, yuppies, generation X — there are lots of different terms to describe what makes a certain generation unique. You are part of the Human Genome Generation, the first generation of people to have access to the entire DNA sequence of human genes. And how will that change your life? That depends on the scientific curiosity and hard work of the scientists of your generation.

Will the development of GM salmon destroy wild Atlantic salmon like these or will they provide more and less expensive fish for people to eat? What do you think about this hot fishy debate?

they could displace the wild fish, pushing them out of their natural environments. This is already a serious problem with farmed salmon, and some people believe the case of GM fish will be even more extreme.

However, those in favor of approving GM salmon say there are ways to ensure that GM salmon do not escape — and making sure that, if they do, they cannot breed with wild relatives. Aqua Bounty plans to create and sell only sterile females that do not lay eggs, so there will be no cross-breeding. The company also says that escapes could be prevented by keeping GM fish farms in inland pools rather than in underwater coastal pens. The governments who represent you are currently deciding this issue. What would you advise them to do?

Do Mutants Really Exist?

Strange combinations of human and animal species inhabit comic books and Hollywood movies — Spider-man, werewolves, the Fly, Teenage Mutant Ninja Turtles — but do such creatures really exist? In 1980, scientists at Yale University in the US became the first in history to

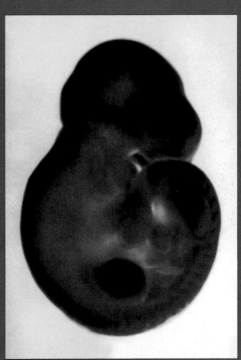

implant a human gene successfully in another species — a mouse. Although mice with human brains or phenomenal powers may be the stuff of fiction, transgenic mice are having an incredible impact on medical science. They've helped scientists develop the first vaccine against Lyme disease. Transgenic mice are also used in the ongoing study of cancer and other major human diseases, such as diabetes, and Alzheimer's, Parkinson's, and Huntington's diseases.

A transgenic mouse fetus. Transgenic mice are being used to help solve medical mysteries.

BARCODER ™

COI Sequence: ACTIVE
GCTATTA

New Species —

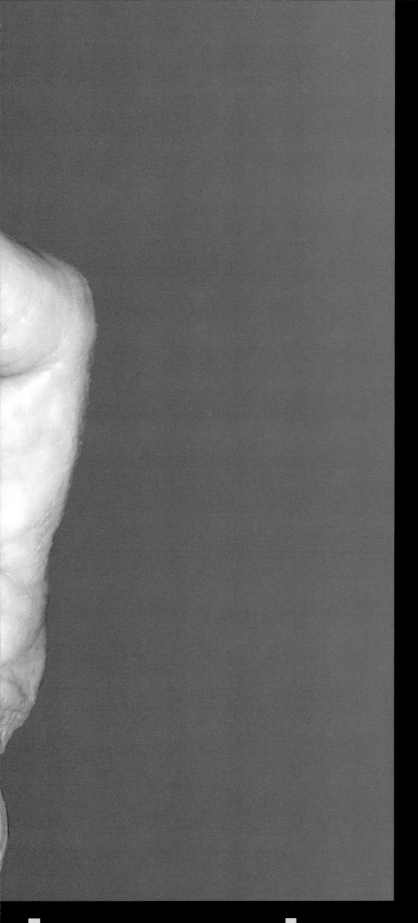

Imagine yourself in the future, taking your own son or daughter for a walk. When your little one bends over to smell a flower or flips over a rock to watch the insects scurry, you're ready with the names of every plant, bug, or beast. All you have to do is pluck a tuft of hair, pinch a piece of leaf, or swat a mosquito. With a quick sweep of your barcoder, you can identify species as easily as a supermarket clerk scans your groceries. A chip the size of your thumbnail carries 30 million species-specific gene sequences. Sound like science-fiction? Turn the page to see into the future.

Handheld DNA barcoder

Into the Future

Pick a BioBlitz

Local scientists enjoy the thrill of doing a BioBlitz with their neighbors.

What on Earth is a BioBlitz? A BioBlitz is a 24-hour, marathon identification session designed to inventory as many species as possible in a park, forest, or section of coastline.

Each year, kids and adults all over the world get together with scientists to BioBlitz. The results are extraordinary. In New York City's Central Park, more than 350 scientists and volunteers crawled on hands and knees, climbed trees, and snorkeled ponds to identify 836 species. A New Zealand crew counted 1,556 species in just two of Aukland's parks. And 1,898 species — including a bounty of parasite species in a dead opossum — were documented in a 265-hectare (654-acre) park in the US state of Connecticut.

While some scientists enjoy the thrill of doing a BioBlitz with their neighbors, hundreds of others have formed a worldwide network to achieve the awesome goal of naming and classifying every species on Earth. The scientists who make up the ALL Species Foundation are determined to discover the entire encyclopedia of life within the next 25 years.

For Jean-Marc Moncalvo, being a part of the ALL Species Foundation means studying tiny things. Jean-Marc is fascinated by microorganisms. Life on a microscopic scale is

BioBlitzing a pond in Central Park, New York.

much more diverse than the world we can see. Yet studying these strange organisms is so challenging that they remain the least understood life forms in the world. Often half the species Jean-Marc finds when he travels to the tropics are new species.

Jean-Marc says you could take samples anywhere and always find microbes. The rust spots on the leaves of your garden plants are actually microscopic fungi. The dust that causes allergies is a collection of microorganisms. Whether you travel to Thailand or Mexico for a vacation, or spend your time in your school yard, new species of microbes are there to be found.

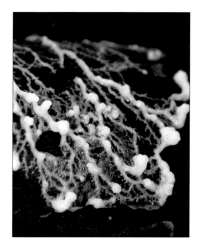 

Jean-Marc Moncalvo is developing a classification system for the strange organisms known as slime molds. During its blobby plasmodial phase (left), a slime mold gorges on its prey of bacteria, spores, and even other slime molds until it runs out of food. Then, travelling at 1 millimetre (0.04 in.) per hour, it lifts itself up a stump and sprouts fruiting bodies (right) that may resemble shimmering, miniature colorful soccer balls atop toothpick stalks, or maybe tiny chocolate ice-cream cones.

RESEARCHER PROFILE

Jean-Marc Moncalvo

Jean-Marc loved to read books about new discoveries when he was a kid— the adventures of Marco Polo, the discovery of electricity, the wonders of space exploration. Today he is still really curious about everything. Jean-Marc loves to look at and experience new things, especially learning about microorganisms that few people have seen, and even fewer have studied. Jean-Marc is an evolutionary biologist who works for the University of Toronto and the Royal Ontario Museum.

HOT DEBATE   HOW MANY SPECIES LIVE ON PLANET EARTH?

Based on the number and location of species described by science so far, some scientists estimate that the total number of species living on our planet is 5 million. Others claim the number is closer to 100 million! Surprisingly, scientists have a better understanding of how many stars there are in the galaxy than how many species there are on Earth.

The Future of Life

Does the future of the search for new species — the future of life on Earth — look bright? The excitement of all these wonderful discoveries is mixed with worry about how species are threatened by climate change, loss of habitat, over-harvesting, and other environmental problems.

What's the best way to conserve species, new and old? Think back to all the people you met in this book. They each make their own contribution to that goal. Their lives are committed to understanding the amazing life that exists on Earth, and to identifying the richest, most diverse places where species are found. They share their knowledge and ask for help in protecting the wonders they know. There is still so much to be learned and celebrated.

Linked to a GPS (global positioning system) and a central computer, this handheld barcoder will provide instant access to a species' identity, its exact location, and all the natural history information available on the World Wide Web. ▼

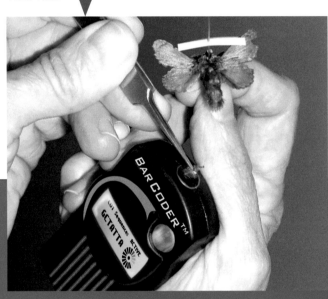

Unlocking the Barcode

Paul Hebert, a scientist at the University of Guelph in Canada, believes his Barcode of Life project will make it possible to identify every animal species in Canada within the next ten years. With the total number of species on our planet estimated to be somewhere between 5 and 100 million, Paul argues that trying to identify organisms by their appearance is too complex. It would be better to identify species by using their own unique DNA sequences.

The scientists involved in Paul's Barcode of Life project are developing the technology to quickly recover a species barcode, read its DNA sequence, and match it against the barcode library of what will eventually contain every species on Earth. Ultimately, the Barcode of Life project will revolutionize the way we identify life. In 250 years since Linnaeus invented his system to classify life, scientists have identified only 2% of the Earth's species. Paul is hoping to speed up that process dramatically.

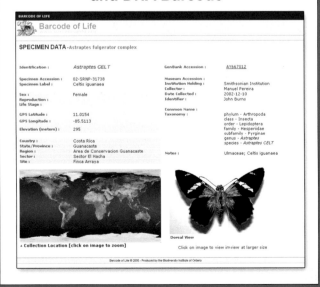

Web-Accessible Specimen Data and DNA Barcode

Paul Hebert

Paul's earliest childhood memory was collecting an insect. When he dashed into the house to show his mother the bee he had trapped within a glass jar, he suddenly tripped. The glass broke, Paul cut himself, blood squirted out, and the boy was utterly convinced he was going to die. Luckily, the cut healed quickly, and the bee escaped. Paul had gained an immediate passion for small forms of life. Paul's genetics research lab is based at the University of Guelph.

A Tree of Life

How are the species identified by the ALL Species Foundation, the BioBlitzes, or the Barcode of Life related? This question drives the scientists working together on the Tree of Life Web Project. Each Web page provides information about one group of organisms. The pages are linked to one another in the form of an up-to-date evolutionary tree that connects all species.

You might be surprised at how little we know about life on Earth. Most species — even species we depend on for food, clothing, and preventing disease — are poorly understood. The Tree of Life marks the beginning of an extraordinary new age of understanding Earth's species.

The Last Word

This has been such a wonderful book to write. More new species are being discovered now than at any other time in history. Each time I thought I was finished, I'd find out about another new species to include in the book. I enjoyed the lively discussions between scientists about whether or not a species really is new. The information is changing so quickly, some of the scientists I spoke with when I began the research for the book had changed their interpretations of their work by the time the book was being published. So the stories you find in these pages have changed many times, and will no doubt change again — and again — as scientists learn more and different things about new species. That's what I find so exhilarating about science, a field rich with creative ideas, multiple viewpoints, and hot debates. You never know how or when or where something you think is a fact may turn out to be not so certain after all, and the thrill of new discovery begins again.

— Elin Kelsey

Acknowledgments

Special thanks go to all of the scientists who helped to create this book. They shared fascinating stories, helped to explain tough scientific concepts, donated photographs, and reviewed the text to make sure it was based on the most up-to-date scientific ideas. These generous and thoughtful people include Robert Anderson, Canadian Museum of Nature; Loren Reiseberg, Indiana University, US; Robert Murphy, Royal Ontario Museum, Canada; Don Colgan, Australian Museum; Mark Robbins, University of Kansas, US; Paul Hebert, University of Guelph, Canada; Kelly Decker and Lynn Rothschild, NASA-Ames Research Center, US; Diane Poehls, Woods Hole Oceanographic Institute, US; John Hare, Wild Camel Protection Foundation, England; David Hillis, University of Texas at Austin, US; Edward Seidel, Marine Resources Aquarium of the Maine Department of Resources, US; Michael Fay, Royal Botanical Gardens Kew, England; Bonnie Baxter, Westminster College, US; Ian MacDonald, Texas A&M University, US; Ernest Cooper, WWF Canada; Kathleen Londry, University of Manitoba, Canada; Arne Mooers and Christine Parent, Simon Fraser University, Canada; Stephen Palumbi, Hopkins Marine Station of Stanford University, US; Alan McHughen, University of California, Riverside, US; Jean-Marc Moncalvo, University of Toronto, Canada; Frank Ruddle, Yale University, US; Jim Barry, Monterey Bay Aquarium Research Institute, US; Colin Malcolm, University of London, England; and Jason Grant, University of Nuechatel, Switzerland. I am particularly grateful to Marc van Roosmalen for his inspiring conversations from the Brazilian Amazon, and for writing such a lovely foreword to the book.

Thanks to Sheba Meland for inviting me to write this book. And to Anne Shone and Kat Mototsune for their masterful editing and crafting of the final product. Great appreciation to Victoria Hill for filling the book with captivating photographs and images, and to Blair Kerrigan for his artistry and enthusiasm in design.

Warmest thoughts go to all kids who share a love of nature and science, and of reading and writing. It is a great gift to celebrate the world with you.

Photo Credits

For reasons of space, the following abbreviations are used:

FFI – Fauna & Flora International
MBA – Monterey Bay Aquarium
MBARI – Monterey Bay Aquarium Research Institute
NMNH – National Museum of Natural History
NOAA – National Oceanic & Atmospheric Administration
NURP – National Undersea Research Program
SPL – Science Photo Library
USDA – United States Department of Agriculture
VP – Valan Photos
WHOI – Woods Hole Oceanographic Institute

Cover (top left): Dr. Marc van Roosmalen; (bottom left): John Beatty/SPL; (column from top to bottom): © 2005 Harbor Branch Oceanographic Institution; MBA; Robert C. Simpson/VP; www.glofish.com; © MBARI; Back Cover (top left): John Beatty/SPL; (column from top to bottom): MBA; © Lisa O'Donnell; Dr. Marc van Roosmalen; Vertebrate Zoology Bird Collection, Canterbury Museum, New Zealand; © 2002 MBARI; Title page: John Beatty/SPL; Page 5: Dr. Marc van Roosmalen; 8 (main): Phil Banko/CORBIS; 8 (inset): Dale C. Spartas/CORBIS; 10 (top): Wayne Lankinen/VP; 10 (bottom): Robert C. Simpson/VP; 11 (top): Aubrey Lang/VP; 11 (middle): John Fowler/VP; 11 (bottom): Robert C. Simpson/VP; 12 (top): J.A. Wilkinson; 12 (middle): Harold V. Green/VP; 12 (bottom): Robert C. Simpson/VP; 13 (top): OAR/ NURP/NOAA; 13 (bottom): Dr. Robert W. Murphy; 14 (left): Matthew Oldfield, Scubazoo/SPL; 14 (right): CCI Archives/SP; 15 (top): Miss Wedgwood of Leith Hill Place; 15 (bottom left): John Beatty/SP; 15 (bottom right): Private Collection; 16: Alfred Pasieka/SP; 17 (top): James D. Markou/VP; 17 (bottom): Don Roberson; 18 (main): Frans Lanting/Minden Pictures; 19 (inset): Dr. Marc van Roosmalen; 20: Dr. Marc van Roosmalen; 21 (top left): Dr. Marc van Roosmalen; 21 (bottom left): David Haring/Duke University Primate Center; 21 (right): Sygma/CORBIS; 22–23 (all but lizard on a dime): Dr. Robert W. Murphy; 23 (lizard on a dime): S. Blair Hedges; 24: Robert M. Peck; 25 (top): Louis Swift; 25 (bottom): Robert M. Peck; 26: Robert M. Peck; 27 (top): Robert M. Peck; 27 (bottom): M. Robbins/VIREO; 28: courtesy U.S. National Fish and Wildlife Forensics Laboratory; 29 (top): courtesy U.S. National Fish and Wildlife Forensics Laboratory; 29 (bottom left): Dave Taylor; 29 (bottom right): M. Maylvahanan/VP; 30 (top): courtesy Dr. Robert Anderson; 30 (bottom): Chip Clark/NMNH; 31 (top); Prof. Stewart B. Peck; 31 (bottom): courtesy Dr. Robert Anderson; 32: courtesy Dr. Robert Anderson; 33 (top): courtesy Dr. Robert Anderson; 33 (bottom left): Ray Crundwell/University of London; 33 (bottom right): Peter Frank © 2004 Canadian Museum of Nature; 34 (main): © 2005 Harbor Branch Oceanographic Institution; 35 (inset): MBA; 36 (top): Rolf Gradinger; 36 (middle): Kevin Raskoff; 36 (bottom): Bodil Bluhm; 37 (Big Red, top): © 2002 MBARI; 37 (Big Red, bottom): © 2002 NOAA/MBARI; 37 (middle right): © MBARI; 37 (Earth): courtesy of Earth Sciences and Image Analysis Laboratory, NASA Johnson Space Center/AS17-148-22727/http://eol.jsc.nasa.gov; 37 (bottom): © 2005 Harbor Branch Oceanographic Institution; 38: Kim Fulton-Bennett © 2004 MBARI; 39 (top): © 2000 MBARI; 39 (bottom): © 2005 Norbert Wu/www.norbertwu.com; 40 (bottom): © 1998 MBARI; 41 (top left): MBA; 41 (bottom): Randy Wilder/MBA; 42–43: MBA; 44: WHOI; 45 (all but bottom right): WHOI; 45 (bottom right): WHOI; 46 (main): NASA/JPL/Cornell; 47 (inset): Dr. Linda Stannard, UCT/SPL; 48–49: John Hare; 50 (top): Dr. Reinhardt Kristensen; 50 (bottom left): Bernhard Edmaier/SPL; British Antarctic Survey/SPL; 51 (left): Ricki Rosen/CORBIS SABA; 51 (right): P. Rona/OAR/NURP/NOAA; 52–53: courtesy Dr. Bonnie Baxter; 54: CORBIS; 55 (top): Dr. Tony Brain/SPL; 55 (middle): Dr. Linda Stannard, UCT/SPL; 55 (bottom): Dr. Kari Lounatmaa/SPL; 56 (top two): courtesy Dr. Kathleen Londry; 56 (bottom): Dr. Kelly Decker; 57 (top two): courtesy Dr. Kathleen Londry; 57 (bottom): OAR/NURP; 58: NASA/JPL/Cornell; 59 (top): NASA/JSC; 59 (middle): Richard B. Hoover, Elena Pikuta and Asim Bej, NASA MSFC/NSSTC University of Alabama in Huntsville, and the University of Alabama at Birmingham; 60: Chip Clark/NMNH; 61 (inset): Vertebrate Zoology Bird Collection, Canterbury Museum, New Zealand; 62: Vertebrate Zoology Bird Collection, Canterbury Museum, New Zealand; 63 (top): Vertebrate Zoology Bird Collection, Canterbury Museum, New Zealand; 63 (middle): Will Cook/Duke University Biology Department; 63 (bottom): Jeremy Holden/FFI; 64: Dr. Lance Barrett-Lennard; 65 (top): Dr. Lance Barrett-Lennard; 65 (bottom): AFP/S. Shimizu-Ho/Getty Images; 66: Roslin Institute, Edenburgh; 67: courtesy of the College of Veterinary Medicine, Texas A&M University; 68 (bottom): National Archives of Australia A1861, 7750; 68 (top): State Library of Victoria/b15734; 69 (top): Jonathan Blair/CORBIS; 69 (bottom): Fairfaxphotos/36262303; 70 (top): Eric and David Hosking/CORBIS; 70 (bottom): DK limited/CORBIS; 71 (top): Biju Sathyabhama Das/Vrije Universiteit Brussel; 71 (middle): John Cancalosi/VP; 71 (bottom): © Robert M. Peck; 72: courtesy Dr. Christine Parent; 73 (left): REUTERS/Handout; 73 (right): REUTERS/Beawiharta; 74 (main): Sara Cedar Miller/Central Park Conservancy; 75 (inset): www.glofish.com; 76 (bottom): © Jason Rick; 77 (top left): Ken Patterson/VP; 77 (main and insets): © Jason Rick; 77 (bottom): Robert Scheer/Indianapolis Star; 78: © Lisa O'Donnell; 79 (left): courtesy Dr. David Hillis; 79 (right): © Dr. Jason Grant; 80 (inset): courtesy USDA; 80 (main): Scott Bauer/USDA; 81 (left): Lew Robertson/CORBIS; 81 (middle): James R. Page/VP; 81 (right): Wouterloot-Gregoire/VP; 82: www.glofish.com; 83: Phil Schermeister/CORBIS; 84 (left): courtesy AquBounty Technologies, Inc.; 84–85 (middle): G. Van Ryckervorsel/VP; 85: courtesy Yale University, Transgenic Mouse Service; 86 (main): courtesy Biodiversity Institute of Ontario; 87 (inset): John Fowler/VP; 88: Jeff Stolzer/The Explorers Club; 89: courtesy Dr. Jean-Marc Moncalvo; 90: courtesy Biodiversity Institute of Ontario; 91 (top): © Robert Berdan; 91 (bottom): courtesy Biodiversity Institute of Ontario; 92 (author photo): © 2004 Kathryn Kittinger.

Glossary

Antibiotic a drug that kills bacteria

Archaea one of the three major domains of life; Archaea are single-celled microorganisms, many of which live in extreme environments

Astrobiologist a scientist who studies life in the universe

Bacteria one of the three major domains of life; bacteria are single-celled microorganisms

Bacteriologist a scientist who studies bacteria

BioBlitz a 24-hour, marathon session to identify species

Biodiversity the diversity of life on Earth

Bio-ethicist a person who studies and helps to resolve scientific dilemmas

Biological hotspots locations where a very high diversity of species are found

Biologist a scientist who studies forms of life

Botanist a scientist who studies plants

Captive breeding the breeding of species in zoos

Chordate the phylum Chordata (or Chordates) includes all of the vertebrates, as well as a number of marine and seldom-seen organisms that have a stiffening rod but not a true backbone

Cloning a complicated series of technological procedures to produce exact copies of a single gene, cell, or organism

Cryptic species species that look alike but differ genetically

DNA (deoxyribonucleic acid) the chemical inside a cell that carries the genetic instructions for making living organisms

Ecology a branch of biology that studies living things and their environments

Ecosystem a system formed by the inter-relationships between living organisms and their physical environment

Endangered species a species so rare, it is threatened by extinction

Entomologist a scientist who studies insects

Evolution biological change through time

Evolutionary biologist a scientist who studies how species change over time

Extinct species a species that no longer exists

Extraterrestrial life forms of life that may exist beyond planet Earth

Extremophile an organism (usually single-celled and microscopic) that lives in environments so hot, cold, acidic, salty, or highly pressurized that most living things couldn't survive there

Fossil record all of the fossils that have existed throughout the history of life on Earth

Genes pieces of DNA that are located at specific locations in a cell; the fundamental units by which genetic information is transferred from parents to offspring

Genetic engineering the process of changing the genetic makeup of an organism by transferring to it DNA from another organism

Genetically modified organisms (GMOs) plants, animals, or microorganisms whose genetic material (DNA) has been altered to give them desired characteristics

Genetics the study of how traits are passed down from one generation to the next

Geneticist a biologist who specializes in genetics

Geology a science that explores the history of the Earth as recorded in rocks

GPS (global positioning system) a satellite-based navigation system

Herpetologist a scientist who studies amphibians and reptiles

Human Genome Generation the first generation of people living once the DNA sequence of human genes was discovered

Hydrothermal vent a geyser on the deep ocean floor that spews out super-hot, mineral-rich water

Invertebrates animals without backbones

Microorganisms organisms so tiny, they can only be seen through a microscope; also called *microbes*

Molecular systematics the process of using the genetic information carried in molecules to classify life on Earth

Ornithologist a scientist who studies birds

Paleontologist a scientist who studies ancient life

Pangaea the supercontinent that existed on Earth over 200 million years ago

Primatologist a scientist who studies monkeys and other primates

ROV (remotely operated vehicle) an underwater device sent to gather samples and information from great depths

Systematic entomologist a scientist who classifies insects

Taxonomist a biologist who specializes in classifying organisms into groups based on their structure, origin, and behavior

Taxonomy the science of naming and classifying living things

Transgenic species a plant, animal, or other living organism that has had part of another species' genetic code transferred into it through techniques of genetic engineering

Vertebrate any animal with a backbone or spinal column; birds, mammals, fish, amphibians, and reptiles are all vertebrates

Wildlife forensics the science of solving crimes that have been committed against wild animals

New Species on the Web

There is an unbelievable amount of information about new species on the Web — but be warned that some of it is not backed up with real research, and you may come across hoaxes. The sites listed here are ones that I found helpful, full of interesting information, accurate, and fun!

Search for "new species" on the Web, and you'll come up with *millions* of hits. To narrow your search, add the name of the life form you're interested in. For instance, type in "new species bird." Want to know more about the newest new species? Type "new species" and the current year. Once you get a list of hits, scroll down until you spot one of the top on-line science magazines — such as *BBC News, National Geographic, Discovery,* or *New Scientist* — and check out their articles.

There are also lots of great sites specially designed for kids who are interested in the science of life on Earth. Take a look at the Exploratorium's Ten Cool Science Sites for an exciting selection of award winners that both kids and scientists have bookmarked as personal favorites.

Exploratorium: Ten Cool Science Sites
www.exploratorium.edu/learning_studio/cool/life

The GEE! In Genome
nature.ca/genome/

Tree of Life Web Project
tolweb.org/tree/phylogeny.html

Extreme 2000 Voyage to the Deep
www.ocean.udel.edu/deepsea/

eNature Field Guides
www.enature.com/

NASA Astrobiology Institute
nai.arc.nasa.gov/students/index.cfm

Life in Extreme Environments
www.astrobiology.com/extreme.html

All About Birds
www.birds.cornell.edu/programs/allaboutbirds/

University of California, Berkeley: Museum of Palaeontology
www.ucmp.berkeley.edu/

Index